THE TENNIS WORKSHOP

The TENNIS
WORKSHOP

A Complete Game Guide

Alan Jones with Barry Wood

The Crowood Press

First published in 1991 by
The Crowood Press Ltd
Gipsy Lane, Swindon
Wiltshire SN2 6DQ

British Library Cataloguing in Publication Data

Jones, Alan
    The tennis workshop.
    1. Lawn tennis
    I. Title II. Wood, Barry
    796.342

ISBN 1 85223 281 1

Throughout this book the pronouns 'he', 'him' and 'his' have been used
inclusively and are intended to apply to both males and females.

Picture credits

The photographs in this book were kindly supplied by *Allsport*; the black-
and-white sequences were taken by Bob Martin and Gray Mortimore of
Allsport.

The illustrations were drawn by Janet Sparrow.

Typeset by Keyboard Services, Luton

Printed in Hong Kong by South China Printing Co.

ACKNOWLEDGEMENTS

I would like to acknowledge the valuable assistance given by Barry Wood, who has managed to put my thoughts and knowledge into words, and also contributed to this book. Thanks are also due to Jo Durie, Clare Wood and James Lenton for the time they gave for many of the photographs featured throughout the book – and for the work of Bob Martin in taking the pictures.

I would like to thank my close friend John Goodfellow, who has been patient enough to scrutinize the contents of this book many times and correct the grammar and spelling, and Belinda Borneo for her comments and assistance.

I would also like to give special mention to Sonia Davis, former British under-12, under-14 and under-21 National Champion, now retired and living in the US. Without Sonia and her phenomenal dedication and desire to improve, I would never have become a serious tennis coach.

I thank Jo too, for allowing me the privilege to work with a top player, and for the encouragement she has inspired by continuing to play on as a dedicated professional despite serious injury problems during the past couple of years. Her attitude has been a credit to the game.

I am grateful to Stephen Marks of French Connection and Stephen Rubin of Pentland Industries, both of whom were kind enough to help me with the development of my coaching in the early days.

My grateful thanks also go to Pilkington Glass, whose generous sponsorship of several of my players has given us the opportunity to work together. Without their assistance, I would certainly not have been able to follow my pupils' individual development as much as I would have liked.

I have learned a great deal from Lennie Heppell and my thanks go to him also. He has broadened my understanding of the value of proper movement. He shows amazing enthusiasm for a man now in his seventies.

Finally, my greatest debt is to my wife, Vicki, and children, Laura and Ryan. Without their support and encouragement, I would have been unable to travel the world and work at the highest level on the Women's Tour.

CONTENTS

FOREWORD

If you are interested in playing tennis, whether as a beginner or as an experienced professional, you will find this book an important source of instruction and advice.

Written in clear, precise but conversational style, the book covers all aspects of the game, including such often ignored subjects as the right clothing and shoes to wear.

Technique is dealt with in great detail, and you will find a comprehensive range of practice suggestions to go with the text. All aspects of technique are backed up by an excellent selection of photographs and illustrations, which I particularly enjoyed.

The book recognizes that good movement is vital to tennis success. Instruction in this area is provided by Lennie Heppel, an expert in the field. Also essential for peak performance is the proper mental preparation, which is examined from the player's perspective as well as the perspective of the parents of young players.

If you are serious about playing tennis, either as a club player or a professional, this book contains all you will need to get the best out of yourself.

So, enjoy *The Tennis Workshop*, and enjoy your tennis!

Steffi Graf

11

PREFACE

As an avid participant in many sports and as a teacher of one sport, I fervently believe that the enthusiast never ceases in his desire to improve, whether he be a keen youngster or a dedicated veteran.

One of the plus points of tennis is that you can continue playing it right into your twilight years; it is not just a game for the young – it can be enjoyed by everyone and at all levels.

In this book, technique, practice routines, coaching, injury prevention, equipment, court surfaces and the part they play are thoroughly investigated, and short tennis for the youngster is also covered.

The Tennis Workshop also examines the type and level of mobility appropriate for the sport – a topic, which, in my opinion, has never received the attention it deserves. No matter at what level you play your tennis, there is no doubt that you will achieve higher performance by improving your mobility and agility. That theme will be emphasized throughout this book at every stage, since what characterizes the most highly-ranked players of both sexes is that they are all very fast, balanced, mobile machines.

Another aspect of the game which is often grossly under-estimated is the mental approach. Lack of self-confidence is a huge barrier and players at most levels are afraid of making mistakes, but only by making mistakes will you improve.

Whether you are a casual park player, a social club player, or someone aspiring to become an international player, it is impor-tant to appreciate that tennis is a highly competitive game. You should always be seeking to gain an extra edge over your opponent. I hope that within the frame-work of this book I will be able to give that little extra edge to many people.

Do not become obsessed with technique, especially in the early stages of learning. First, master the rudiments of the game, running to the ball and hitting it any way you can. Then, use technique to refine your game. Always remember: there is no best way to learn or play. Everyone will respond to different aspects of teaching and will be more able at one thing than another.

However good this book may be in point-ing you in the right direction in developing your technique, tactics and movement, please be aware that the key to progress is practice, practice, and more practice. With-out doubt, all the players who achieve success at any level are those who spend a great deal of time on the practice court.

If you have never set foot upon a tennis court, if you are a seasoned professional, or if you stand anywhere in-between, I be-lieve that you will benefit from the informa-tion and advice contained within these pages, and, hopefully, I will be able to impart some of the knowledge I have gained in twenty-five years associated with the game.

So, go out on the court, experiment with your game and, most important of all, have fun.

PART 1

INTRODUCTION

1
THE MODERN GAME

Recent Trends

A fine testament to the game is how little the rules and scoring system have changed since the game began. In recent times the foot-fault rule has changed, and in the scoring system (to reduce the length of most matches) a tie-break has been introduced at six games all. These minor modifications reflect an excellent system that has stood the test of time.

However, there has been a tremendous amount of change in the way the game has developed in the last fifteen to twenty years. This has been brought about mainly by two factors. One is the large amount of money that has been introduced in the game. This has naturally encouraged top players to demand a high degree of professionalism from themselves. The second is due to the development of the modern racquet. As recently as ten or fifteen years ago, players were still winning major events with a wooden racquet. The use of different materials such as carbon, fibreglass and graphite has definitely made the racquet easier to manipulate and handle.

Changes in Technique

The development of the racquet has brought about a profound change in the way many of the top professionals play the game.

For many years there were traditionally accepted ways for the player to hold and swing the racquet. Top players now use a very broad spectrum of styles. This is due to the greater range of techniques made available by the use of modern racquets, while each technique is linked to, if not dependent on, the grip that is being used.

The Western grip is now used by many of today's top players, but I personally believe that there is no perfect way to play the game. Looking at the styles used by the top players of recent times (Jimmy Connors, John McEnroe, Ivan Lendl, Bjorn Borg, Stefan Edberg, Mats Wilander, Michael Chang, Pete Sampras, Martina Navratilova, Chris Evert, Steffi Graf, Monica Seles, Jennifer Capriati) they all show special individual traits, and no one player grips the racquet in exactly the same way.

There has to be a common factor which lends itself to top-level play. Technically, it is the way players are able to effectively and repeatedly bring their racquet face to the ball, because this is where – no matter what grip or swing is used – a perfect strike is required. In order to successfully repeat this process, it is evident that good players require early preparation of the racquet and excellent footwork around the ball, i.e. they must create the right positions.

Tactical Developments

Another interesting feature which helps to make tennis such an exciting game is the varying tactics used by the players during their matches. There is the aggressive, hard-hitting, adventurous approach, or the more subtle, defensive and consistent type of play. Some players prefer to play the ball flat; others like to use topspin or slice a great deal. Some serve and volley and will seek to be most effective from the net, others develop a skilful touch-game from the back of the court.

It is up to you to discover which style suits you best and to seek to improve and develop it.

2
BASIC RULES AND SKILLS

If you are an absolute beginner, you will need to know about the following topics.

Scoring

If the server wins four consecutive points, the scoring sequence is as follows: fifteen–love (15–0), thirty–love (30–0), forty–love (40–0), game. Should the receiver win every other point, the sequence would run: fifteen–love (15–0), fifteen–all (15–15), thirty–fifteen (30–15), thirty–all (30–30), forty–thirty (40–30), deuce (40–40). Each player may then reach 'advantage' by winning the next point and, by winning the following point, also win the game.

It follows, then, that a game can only be won by a minimum of two clear points – for instance, to 30 and from deuce.

Similarly, a set, which consists of six games, can only be won by a minimum of two clear games unless the tie-break is in operation – this situation will be examined in a moment. The winner of the set claims a maximum of six games, for example 6–4 or 6–3. However, if the score reaches five games all (5–5), then the set can still be won if one player takes the next two games to 7–5.

Tie-Breaks

The tie-break system has evolved a little over a period of time, but there is no need here to go into the history of its introduction or the way it has changed.

The tie-break will usually come into operation if the score reaches six games all (6–6). In a tie-break situation, the points are counted from one to seven and the first player to reach seven points with a mini-

mum margin of two points, for example 7–5 or 7–3, wins the set seven games to six (7–6). If there is no two-point margin at that stage, the game continues until that margin is achieved, for example 8–6 or 12–10.

In some tournaments the tie-break is not used and the set continues until one of the players achieves a two-game margin, for example 8–6 or 9–7. This may occur in all sets, or just the final set, according to the rules of the individual tournament.

The Bounce and the Court

Beginners should also remember the following: only one bounce of the ball is allowed at all times, although the ball can be hit in the air before the bounce.

In singles, the players are restricted to placing the ball within the area of the court inside the 'tramlines' (*see* Fig 1), but in doubles, players are able to use the entire court area.

The Serve

In both singles and doubles, players serve first from the right-hand court into the opponent's service box area across the net – from the server's left and the opponent's right.

Players are allowed to serve either over- or under-arm, although over-arm is the preferred way because it is more effective and more pace can be put on the ball. Two attempts of serve are given. Most players hit an aggressive first serve and, if that fails, they usually take a little pace off the second serve to ensure a greater degree of accuracy.

15

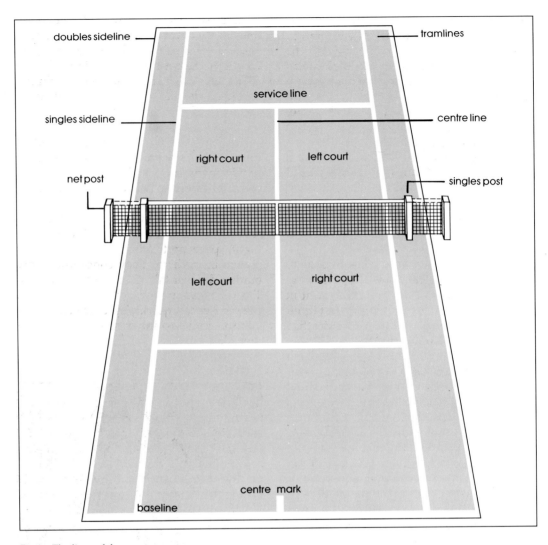

doubles sideline — tramlines

service line

singles sideline — centre line

right court left court

net post singles post

left court right court

centre mark

baseline

Fig 1   The lines of the court.

The top players have learned to put more spin on their serve to support their attack (*see* Chapter 7).

Doubles

In doubles, each player serves once every four games instead of every other game. Everyone serves in rotation and the same players always serve from the same end. However, it is not obligatory, once a set is over, to retain the same order and players can swap their service sequence as the next set begins. Once that decision is taken – and either or both teams can choose to do so – that particular order is retained throughout the set.

During rallies there is no hard and fast rule as to who should take the ball. If you are in a better position than your partner, then there is nothing to prevent you hitting the ball several times in succession.

Equipment

A player needs to use suitable equipment in order to get the best from his game; but be warned: a tennis kit can be costly. However, if you are seriously considering becoming a good player, then you will probably be willing to pay for better-quality equipment. If, however, you cannot afford an expensive kit, do not be deterred: most equipment currently on the market is adequate. Your performance depends more on your ability than your equipment.

One area of equipment that is often overlooked is the balls. In the professional arena they are changed once every seven games, and then after nine games through to the conclusion of the match. Alternatively, the change may occur after the ninth and eleventh games.

It might well seem unnecessary to change balls so frequently when practising, and that is fine, but there is little point in using balls that are obviously past their best. Once they are worn or too soft, they will become difficult to control.

Now go out there and enjoy the participation, then the competition. Never be afraid to experiment with your game; only by trial and error will you improve.

In competition, your aim should be to play to the best of your current level of abilitiy – and hopefully to win. Do not become frustrated when you meet a better player, there will always be one, unless you are the Number One player in the world – and even that does not guarantee success!

Fundamental Principles

These are the basic skills needed to play the game, the responses that need to happen instinctively. To play any ball sport well, sound ball sense linked to agility, footwork and good balance are essential. Tennis, in addition, requires you to co-ordinate the use of racquet work effectively, along with the aforementioned skills.

Ball Sense

Ball sense is the ability to understand the movement of a ball, which enables you to

get in position to execute a shot. You therefore need to understand the flight, speed and direction of the ball and to anticipate where in the court the ball will land. You also need to recognize the type of spin imparted on the ball, the effect this will have, and the likely bounce that will result when the ball strikes the court surface.

Ball sense implies watching the ball. It may sound elementary, but it is an essential requirement. It is worth going to a tournament where good players are performing and to note their early response to the striking of the ball by their opponent. You will realize that their understanding of the flight, pace and direction of the ball is almost immediate. They concentrate very hard and never take their eyes off the ball. The information is passed to the brain, and they move as quickly and effectively as possible into position in order to play their own shot.

Fig 2   Gabriela Sabatini. Note her concentration.

Fig 3   Pete Sampras. Another fine example of concentration. Notice how he is focusing on the ball.

So, as you begin to play tennis, play some mind games of your own and observe how other players prepare for and strike their shots. Try and assess how and where you think the ball will land on the other side of the court.

As your understanding of ball sense develops and you gain some confidence in knowing where the ball will be going, you will then need to work on another essential skill, namely, footwork.

Footwork

The dimensions of a tennis court (*see* Fig 4) demand nimble, positive footwork. Numerous individuals become frustrated in their early days of learning because they cannot co-ordinate moving to the ball and then making the necessary small steps around the ball to create the space needed to strike it.

However, if you are going to enjoy playing the game, I cannot stress enough that

you must gain pleasure, right from the start, out of chasing the ball. Be aware as you learn to play that the quicker you can get to the ball, the more time you will have to prepare and position yourself and execute your shots.

Two basic movements are involved:

1.   Chasing the ball. This will require very strong, almost 'explosive' movements.
2.   Getting into position. This will require small steps which enable you to adjust your footwork and body to put you in the best possible position to play your shot effectively.

Once again, I suggest that you study good players. Notice their alertness, the constant movement of their legs and feet. They are forever adjusting, and these last-moment adjustments are absolutely vital in creating the best possible position to produce the most effective shot.

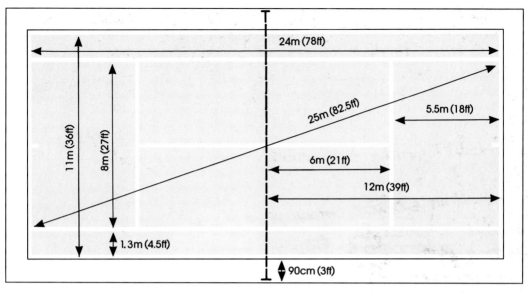

Fig 4   The dimensions of a tennis court.

Balance

Ball sense and good footwork are not enough in themselves. They need to be complemented by a third vital attribute, balance, which is essential in producing consistently effective shots.

Good players make tennis look incredibly easy. They very rarely look awkward, only because they are superbly balanced, mobile athletes.

When studying good players at work, you will note that no matter what position they seem to be in while playing their shots, their shoulders are parallel to the ground. They may be playing a low volley, or a groundstroke with elevation (where they elevate their feet off the ground); they may be in very awkward positions, but they retain their balance.

The non-playing arm plays a very important role. Just prior to the execution of a shot, it helps to create balance and poise. The non-playing arm should never be seen dangling uselessly by a player's side.

Study good players just prior to, during, and immediately after their shot and you will observe how the non-playing arm performs the function of a balancing scale (*see* Fig 5). It helps to create room for the shot,

and almost acts as a guideline for the point at which the ball will be struck in relation to the body, making the shot look more complete and rounded.

The basic skills needed for playing tennis are therefore ball sense, linked to footwork, linked to balance. Once you understand the importance of these three fundamental principles, you can link them to the two most commonly used moving shots that occur in tennis.

Moving Shots

The Groundstroke

The groundstroke is hit as you seek to strike the ball after it has bounced once on the playing surface. It incorporates the fundamental principles previously discussed, whilst the flight, speed and bounce of the ball are also taken into account. You then move to get into position to strike the ball between knee- and waist-height, as the ball is falling from the top of its bounce (*see* Fig 6). This is the most effective height at which to strike the ball for either forehand or backhand groundstrokes.

19

Fig 5   Boris Becker executing a forehand. Note the use of his left arm for balance and poise.

Fig 6   Ivan Lendl in position to strike the ball just below waist-height.

Endeavour at all times to use your footwork in such a way that you are in the position to strike the ball at a consistent and regular height. This will give you the confidence to develop and 'groove' your groundstrokes.

A good way of initiating pressure on the opposition is by taking what is termed an 'early ball'. As you start to improve and gain confidence in striking the ball as it is falling, experiment and actually try to take the ball earlier, before it has reached the top of its bounce (*see* below).

Fig 7   Mats Wilander perfectly illustrates the taking of an early ball.

The Volley

The other moving stroke in tennis is the volley, and this is where you strike the ball before it hits the court. Naturally, you will find yourself using this shot when you are closer to the net. You will be using less

racquet work, and because you are closer to your opponent, you will require quicker reactions and faster movements to get into position. You should be looking to use your understanding of ball sense to get into an ideal position to strike the ball just below shoulder-height.

Try to use your footwork to get into a regular and constant position to strike the ball. On developing a regular stroke you will then be in a position to control the flight and direction of your own shot.

You should now be understanding the movement of the ball better, and getting into position to consistently produce regular shots.

Racquet Control

Another important factor is being able to control the movement of the racquet before impact, upon impact and after the shot. Because of the wide range of shots used in tennis – from exceedingly delicate volleys to extreme topspin lobs – you require many different manipulations of the racquet.

It is the movement of the racquet, the preparation of the swing and the movement both at impact and after the stroke which will determine the speed of the ball, its flight and direction.

Treat the racquet as an extension of your arm. Be comfortable with the support of the racquet in your playing hand; do not strangle the grip. Hold the racquet lightly, and this will help develop a feel of how the racquet reacts at impact.

It is imperative that you find a comfortable grip of the racquet, and obviously, the sooner you can determine the grip you require for the shot you wish to execute, the sooner will you be able to prepare the correct movement (with arms, feet and body) to meet the ball.

However, as you execute your shot, you should also control the racquet face – the angles you create with your racquet face will, of course, determine the destiny of the ball (*see* Fig 8).

Control of the racquet face at impact is

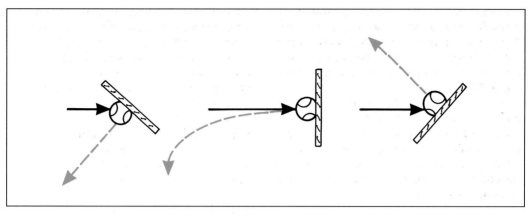

Fig 8 Racquet face angles.

therefore of the utmost importance, and it is the ability to consistently produce the correct movement of the racquet with the correct control of the racquet face which will lead to consistent ball strikes.

The position of the racquet face is determined by the grip of the racquet, so that you create the required angle for whichever shot you wish to execute. It is your hand that will take up the grip, so be aware of the need for good hand-control.

At the same time, changing wrist angles will also affect the racquet face at impact. Do not be afraid to experiment – this is a fun area to explore. It is obvious that too much of an open racquet face will cause the ball to rise upwards, whereas a closed racquet face will cause the ball to play down and into the net.

Before we go on to study the basic techniques applied by all players, let us recap the basic skills needed to play tennis well. These are:

1. Ball sense.
2. Footwork.
3. Balance.
4. Control of the racquet through movement.
5. Control of the racquet face.

If these five fundamental principles are applied properly, they will lead to the development of another essential feature of

all good tennis players, which is the timing of their strokes.

Readiness to Receive in Rallies

The ready position should be achieved between each shot, prior to the preparation of the particular stroke you are about to execute, and is an essential tool in the formation of your stroke. It enables you to prepare for your shot from a regular base.

You should assume the following position: with your feet astride, just beyond shoulder-width apart, lean forward slightly from the waist with your knees slightly bent (see Fig 9).

If you are playing at the baseline, you should stand approximately 60–90cm (2–3ft) behind it, and if at the net you should be approximately 1½–2m (5–7ft) from the net. At all times, keep physically relaxed but mentally alert, and it is advisable to support the racquet at throat-height very lightly, in your non-playing hand.

I would suggest that when at the net you support the racquet a little higher than you do at the baseline. The obvious reason for this is that the majority of volleys will be played about shoulder-height. If you are double-handed you will probably start with your non-playing hand a little further down the grip.

23

Fig 9   Steffi Graf well balanced and ready to move in any direction.

Fig 10   Andre Agassi – note the open stance and
racquet head below the ball, ready to impart topspin.

court. I ask them if they really understand
the angles . . .

According to where you stand on the
court, where you strike the ball from and
where you strike the ball to – and assuming
that the shot is of a certain quality – you
should be able to move into a position
which will protect the likely return of your
shot, anticipating where your opponent
will strike the ball.

This is what I call 'knowing your angles';
understanding the direction, flight, pace
and placement of the ball. It is certainly
an area with which good players are at
ease. They always appear to know where
the ball is going to go. They do too, but
by moving to a certain position on the
court they are at the same time forcing the
opponent to hit the ball into a certain area.
They might also tempt their opponent to
try and hit the ball into a difficult area,
because – according to the position in
which they are standing – there are only
certain places into which their opponent
can hit the ball effectively.

If you think of the ebb and flow that takes
place in a rally, you will realize that it is a
skill that good players put into practice
effectively.

Study the good players. Watch how they
position themselves for each shot. If you
can learn to understand your angles well
and move early and effectively, you will
feel less vulnerable and so more comfortable and confident during your matches.

Understand Your Angles

Players sometimes come to tell me that they
seem to hit the ball reasonably well,
they move well, they can rally and they
are consistent, and yet something is not
right. They feel uncomfortable on the

3
THE TENNIS KIT

Racquets

There has been a tremendous transformation in the range of materials used in the manufacture of racquets. The market used to be dominated by wood, then manufacturers turned to aluminium and metal racquets, and today the bulk of the market is dominated by combinations of fibreglass, carbon and graphite.

One of the biggest assets of playing with these new materials is that – providing you are using the racquet with the correct grip and the right weight – they are considered to be much kinder to the arm and shoulder, thus reducing the risk of tendinitis in shoulder, elbow and wrist joints. These racquets are also much easier to manoeuvre, which explains why players are able to produce whippy topspins, almost like table-tennis players.

The racquet will either be flexible or stiff, according to the percentage of graphite used – the higher the percentage, the stiffer the racquet – and the powerful players will favour the stiffer type of racquet. If you are a wristy type of player, then the more flexible racquet is more likely to suit your game.

The other major development in the manufacture of racquets has been to do with size. The traditional size of racquet – that used in the early days of tennis – has become almost non-existent today. In the early 1980s, the big-headed racquet appeared to be making huge inroads on the market. However, it now appears that the mid-size racquet is favoured (*see* below).

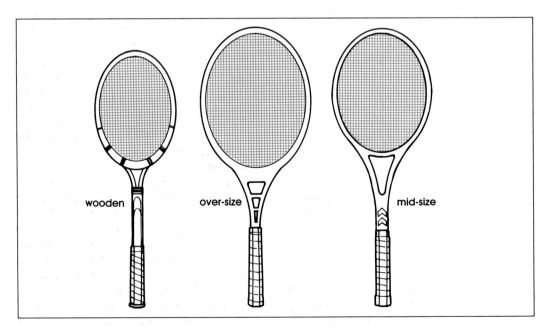

wooden   over-size   mid-size

Fig 11   Racquet sizes.

The greatest merit of the mid-size frame is that the slight reduction in size allows you more manoeuvrability with the racquet head, and I am fairly confident that the mid-size frame is the racquet of the future.

There will always be a market for the large-headed racquet, however. It is certainly helpful to the senior citizen, who, in his advancing years, places less importance on racquet head speed. The merit of the larger racquet is that its bigger face area gives the poor volleyer additional confidence in his net game. Its greatest drawback is in service, where it is difficult to promote as much racquet head speed as desired – an all-important feature of an effective service. The mid-size racquet, on the other hand, allows you to generate the racquet head speed required for aggressive serving.

Grips

The texture of grips has also been subject to change recently. For many years, the traditional leather grip was thought to be kinder to the hand than any other texture. It was soft and absorbed perspiration. However, during long rallies, the leather grip was always prone to moisture-retention. That is why many players would rub sawdust on their hands to ensure a better grip.

Today, two new grips are favoured, both of which are rubber-based. The more common of the two consists of a very thin grip which you simply wrap round the existing leather one. It will probably only last for thirty to fifty hours' use, but it deals more effectively with perspiration and thus prevents the racquet from slipping. The second type of grip consists of the same outer layer as the first one, but includes a cushioned base which replaces the leather grip entirely.

Strings

For many years gut was the most common material used in the manufacture of strings and many tournament players still favour it. Stringing used to be a specialized craft,

done by hand, but there are now highly sophisticated stringing machines with electronic tensioning mechanisms. This has encouraged the development of synthetic stringing and the improvement has been dramatic. Some fifty per cent of the top players are now using the new materials.

The major differences between gut and synthetic strings are cost – a top gut re-string could cost twice as much as the equivalent synthetic one – and performance. Gut is undoubtedly more sensitive than synthetic, and it stands to reason that gut is better for your game. However, it is also more sensitive to climatic conditions – moisture, humidity, dampness and extreme heat – and it is therefore less durable, and thus more costly, than synthetic materials.

Synthetic strings have improved enormously, and many are now available which would appear to have a similar performance to gut. One way in which you can make the synthetic string more sensitive is by having it strung much tighter than you would gut.

Tension

I am often asked by players what tension they should have in their racquet. It really is a question of personal choice, but there is one yardstick I would use: the more aggressive your style of play, the tighter the string, because the ball will tend to fly more. If you like to 'play' with the ball (and by that I mean if you like to keep the ball on the string longer), then I suggest a slackly-strung racquet, because it creates a 'trampoline' effect.

Again, it is really a matter of personal preference. There is a tremendous range of tensions used, even among the top players and some players will have their racquets strung differently according to the surface on which they are playing. Tight strings are sometimes preferred on the faster surfaces, as opposed to the slacker strings used on slower surfaces such as clay – where players have more time at their disposal and feel that they can 'play' with the ball.

Fig 12

Fig 13   Arantxa Sanchez-Vicario – down but not out!

avoid muscular injury caused by exercising in cold conditions.

Professional Advice

Fashion has certainly made its mark as the game has grown in popularity, which means that there is now a baffling range of racquets and other equipment from which to choose.

My advice is to seek out professional help and find out about the racquet that will suit your game, the strings that will suit your style of play and the tension at which they should be strung, as well as the type of shoe you should wear on a particular surface.

I would avoid purchasing your equipment from high street shops. Their sole purpose is to sell their goods. Professionals in your club shop will be able to advise you as they should have a proper understanding of your requirements. They are the experts, and remember it is your body, your game, perhaps your career you are dealing with and it is vitally important that you get it right.

PART 2

TECHNIQUE

4

GRIPS

In the last twenty years or so, the game of tennis has evolved a great deal, so that so-called conventional methods of play have now become old-fashioned and the grip (the way you hold the racquet) has also been subject to change.

One of the main reasons behind this evolution is the fact that two of the major tournaments on the tennis circuit – the US and Australian Opens – have switched from grass courts to other surfaces (*see* Chapter 27). This, in turn, has meant that build-up tournaments have also changed.

We once had a circuit with about twenty-five grass tournaments a year, and this, I believe encouraged a certain style of play and a certain type of grip. On grass courts, you have little time available to change your grip between shots because of the swift pace of the game. Because of the very surface, the ball invariably stays low and skids through particularly quickly, so that the time factor for players to produce their strokes is minimal. (The substitute surfaces used for the Australian and US Opens, together with the preceding tournaments, allow you more time to produce your groundstrokes.)

It therefore follows that if you were to pursue a tennis career which meant playing a high percentage of your tournaments on grass, you would need to use those grips that were the most effective on

Fig 14 Pete Sampras playing a classic lifted backhand.

that surface. Grass courts require you to play an attacking game, where as little grip change as possible is beneficial, and this is still the case today.

There were two commonly used grips – the conventional Eastern grip, as it is known today, which necessitated a small change to the backhand grip, and the Continental grip, which was especially used by many of the fine players of yesteryear.

The lesser number of tournaments played on grass, plus an abundance of players from 'clay court countries' – where Western grip forehands have been used successfully for years – have encouraged many more players to develop their game using this particular style; playing from the back of the court with more time to change the grip (*see* Fig 22).

It is probably worth adding at this point that very few women have played successfully with the Continental grip. The reason is quite simply that men are much stronger in their forearm and wrist area, and this strength allows them to play forehands using this grip. (Ironically, one of the best players of all time, Martina Navratilova, has played successfully using the Continental grip.)

Coupled with the change in court surfaces is the development of the tennis racquet (*see* Chapter 3, page 26). The lighter racquets now available are much easier to manipulate than their wooden equivalents, and the kind of grip you use matters a lot less because of this. The modern racquet allows you to develop your own instinctive style much more readily, rather than relying on 'pure' strokes and 'technical perfection'.

A third factor to consider is the youth element. More people are starting to play from a younger age – this, no doubt, due to the development of the game and the interest it has generated.

When children between the ages of seven and ten start to play, their arms and wrists are not strong enough, so they

Fig 15   The unique Monica Seles, left-handed and double-handed on both sides.

Fig 16   Monica Seles preparing for a two-fisted forehand. Note the weight is on her back foot.

Fig 17   Pete Sampras preparing to strike a forehand. Notice the balance and poise and how the weight is on the back foot.

tend to hold the racquet to hit their forehands with a Western grip. For them, it is quite simply the easiest and most effective way to produce good forehands. For the same reason, and despite the lighter racquets, very few youngsters can physically cope with a single-handed backhand – which explains why the double-handed player has become more prominent in recent years.

These, I believe, are the basic areas which have led to changes in grip styles.

When you start to play and begin competing seriously, you should use a grip that feels totally natural. The racquet does not demand that you play in any particular fashion.

However, a good understanding of the grips currently being used will enable you to develop your own style.

The Eastern Grip
Fig 18

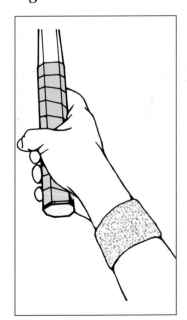

Fig 18   Eastern grip.

This has been the traditional grip for many years, encouraged to be used for the forehand side of the racquet.

Hold the racquet at its throat in the non-playing hand. Take the playing hand to the face of the racquet, bring it down to the grip and shake hands with it.

The benefit of the Eastern grip is that it acts as an extension of your hand, with the palm behind the handle. It has generally been perceived over the years as the grip with which to achieve the maximum weight of shot.

The Western Grip
Figs 20 and 21

The other natural forehand grip is the Western grip, which was virtually taboo until Bjorn Borg became a phenomenal success. It is quite amazing, since he arrived on the scene, how many players throughout the world are now using this grip very successfully.

To obtain the Western grip, simply pick up a racquet as it lays flat and wrap your fingers and thumb around the handle.

Fig 19   The colourful Andre Agassi, here using an extreme Western forehand grip.

Ironically, players have come to use that grip in an even more extreme fashion, so that what was called a Western grip fifteen years ago is probably now termed as a Semi-Western grip (see Fig 20).

The proper Western grip today is held further under the handle (see Fig 21). The merits of the Western grip are that it

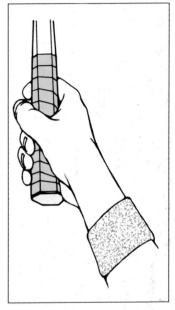

Fig 20   Semi-Western grip.

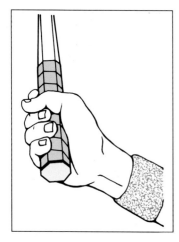

Fig 21   Western grip.

encourages a player to attack the ball above waist-height, and it is probably the most effective way of producing topspin.

On the other hand, since the palm of the hand rests so far below the handle, it is very difficult to impart slice or backspin.

The Continental or Backhand Grip Figs 23 and 24

The three grips previously mentioned – the Eastern, the Western and the Semi-Western are the most commonly used for forehands. However, as we discussed earlier, the Continental grip (*see* Fig 23), which is in essence a backhand grip, can also be used.

The Continental grip has stood the test of time for the good reason that it is very difficult to hit a backhand successfully with an extreme forehand grip, or even with a conventional forehand grip. The strength of the forearm and wrist just does not allow forehand grips to be successful in producing backhand strokes.

To find the backhand grip, use the traditional forehand grip (placing the hand on the face of the racquet, sliding it

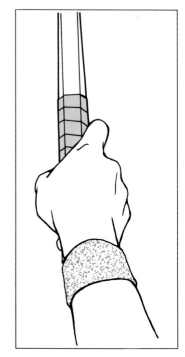

Fig 23   Continental grip.

down and shaking hands with it). Once you have that grip, turn the racquet hand in towards the body a quarter turn. This is the backhand grip, which is incidentally very similar to the Continental grip.

For that reason, players of yesteryear found that they did not need to vary their grip and were quite happy to use the Continental grip – even though it meant that their forehand was probably weaker than their backhand. It was still a small price to pay for the benefit of having to make a minimal grip change on the fast surfaces.

The conventional backhand grip is universally used, although there may sometimes be some slight variation, caused by the placement of the thumb. The majority of players will wrap their thumb around the grip, but others will put their thumb diagonally up the racquet to give greater stability (*see* Fig 24).

Fig 22   Gabriela Sabatini – a fine example of a successful Western-grip player.

36

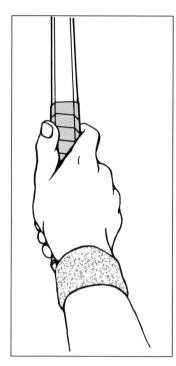

Fig 24   Continental grip with thumb up the handle.

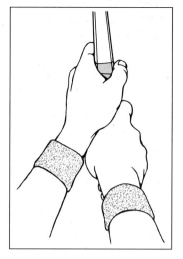

Fig 25   Two-handed backhand grip.

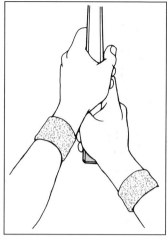

Fig 26   Two-fisted backhand grip.

This backhand grip is universally used because greater strength is created by putting the grip behind the handle. It also allows excellent flexibility and encourages all forms of shot-making, whether flat, topspin or slice.

Because the modern racquet is easier to manipulate, several leading players have become more extreme with their backhand grips; reflected in the fact that there are many more topspin backhands being played now than there were ten years ago.

The Two-Handed Backhand Grip Fig 25

The two-handed backhand grip is obtained as follows: the playing hand makes an orthodox single-handed backhand grip and the non-

playing hand makes an orthodox Eastern forehand grip. You then merge the two hands close together. The obvious merit of holding the racquet with two hands is increased strength, which in turn leads to greater power, linked to greater speed of racquet use.

There are two variations on the backhand grip.

The Two-Fisted Grip

In order to find this grip, place both hands on the racquet with Eastern grips – that is, two strong forehand grips (*see* Fig 26). The best player to date to demonstrate this is Jimmy Connors.

One of the strengths of this particular grip is that it encourages the player to be very aggressive, almost punching at the ball. It creates a very flat stroke with an element of underspin, and this kind of grip promotes an adventurous style of play.

The Inter-Locking Grip

This grip is very rarely used, but as the name suggests, it is

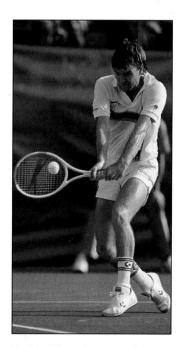

Fig 27   Jimmy Connors – the best exponent of the two-fisted grip.

achieved by linking the two hands together, interlocking the little finger of the playing hand with the index finger of the other.

37

The Service Grip
Fig 28

The service grip is generally recognized as being held the same way by everyone (although variations do, of course, exist).

The service grip is commonly known as the chopper grip. You obtain the grip, as the name suggests, by literally getting hold of the racquet as if you would chop wood with it.

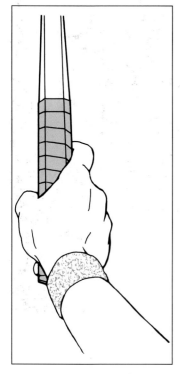

Fig 28   Service (chopper) grip.

The great assets of using the chopper grip are that it enables you to obtain greater racquet head speed; it provides the facility for several service variations, and because it allows for the wrist to be flexible, you can produce not only flat serves but also topspin and slice.

I should stress at this stage that when players are first

confronted with the chopper grip, they find it very difficult to serve with any real effectiveness. It probably means that they are accustomed to serving with the 'frying pan', or forehand grip. That is perfectly adequate for pure out-and-out flat serving. But unfortunately the 'frying pan' will not allow for any wrist manipulation. It is therefore totally unsuitable for developing a second serve, which is dependent on spin and can only be imparted with a flexible wrist.

Many players become frustrated while trying to adapt to a chopper grip, but I can quite categorically state that it is a must if a service is to be developed to its full potential.

Grips for the Smash and Volley

While we are discussing the service it is worth mentioning the smash, because the smash relies on the same mechanics as the service. It therefore requires the same grip, i.e. the chopper grip (*see* Fig 28).

As for the other forecourt shot – the volley – many coaches advocate that beginners use the traditional Eastern forehand grip and the traditional backhand grip. I personally feel that because there is so little time to prepare shots at the net, no matter what standard you are, you should seek out the chopper

grip for volleying.

I must clarify at this stage that there will be a slight accommodation of the grip whether you play a forehand or a backhand volley. By this I mean that the grip change is so minimal that it will not occur consciously. It will just slot in as you favour your backhand or forehand volley.

Any Grip is a Good Grip

We have now covered all the grips that are required to play tennis. Before moving on to discuss how to get the best out of them, it is worth pointing out that in recent times there has been a shift of views within the coaching fraternity.

Coaches used to be very dogmatic and rigid in their opinions about the grips players should use. Yet players such as Ivan Lendl, Mats Wilander, John McEnroe, Jimmy Connors, Pete Sampras, Steffi Graf, Chris Evert, Martina Navratilova and Monica Seles are so diverse in the grips they use that the general feeling amongst the coaches I meet on the professional circuit is that any grip that suits a particular player is a good grip.

That theory applies even though the grip may not look right to the coach and the player looks awkward. If the end-product is successful, then the grip has to be good.

Which Grip to Use?

As discussed earlier, the benefit of an extreme Western grip forehand is that it enables you to produce heavy topspin and also enables you to take the ball above waist-height. However, because of the extreme change from forehand to backhand grip, you will be more vulnerable when playing on faster surfaces. Obviously, this is because you will have less time to change grip. Western-grip players have a tendency to feel less happy at the net because they are unaccustomed to using the simple volley grip. They also struggle to hit down the line off their forehand as effectively as they do cross-court.

The Western grip's greatest advantage is that, because of the excessive topspin that can be imparted on the medium to slow surfaces, you are more capable of pinning your opponent back on the baseline. This means you become a very difficult player to attack.

If you feel more comfortable using the Continental grip, you must understand that you are going to be a more effective net player than a backcourt player. Therefore, seek to develop your tennis around the serve and volley and net-attack game plan, and naturally seek out tournaments that are played on faster surfaces.

A Western-grip player, on the other hand, will play most of his tennis from the back of the court. So, obviously, the way you want to play will influence the grip that you use.

This applies to both men and women, because in recent years the latter have certainly become much more professional, stronger and athletic, and are therefore capable of using any of the grips mentioned.

Fig 29   Pete Sampras – the youngest ever US Open winner.

Likewise, the grip a youngster uses as he starts to play the game will probably influence the way in which he will perform throughout his playing days.

If a player shows a definite aptitude for net-play, a coach would encourage him to come away from the Western grip, even if the player found it natural, because, eventually, the less grip change needed, the better the volley game.

Similarly, if a young player displays a preference for the back of the court, but likes using the Continental grip, it would be wise to encourage him to change to a more conventional or a Semi-Western grip forehand.

I do not believe that Western-grip players could have got very far years ago because the circuit revolved around grass, and they would have found it tough to win

39

Double-Handed Play

The double-handed backhand is here to stay, and with the recent emergence of the mercurial Monica Seles, who plays with not only a double-handed backhand, but also with an extremely efficient double-handed forehand, who is to say what the future holds?

Seles managed to reach the top 10 at the age of fifteen, although many would have discouraged her from playing double-handed off both sides. By succeeding – against the odds, if you like – she has proved that there are different ways to play tennis at the highest level.

One very impressive feature of Seles's game is her early taking of the ball. She stands inside the baseline eighty-five per cent of the time. By doing so, she takes the ball earlier than most and hits it extremely hard.

Because she is double-handed on both sides, she would have to cover much more court if she stood further back and behind the baseline. Her opponents would then be able to use the angles against her. By hitting the ball so hard and hitting it as early as she does, she puts herself in the initiating role. She tends to be in command of most rallies, which again prevents her footwork from being exposed. There is no doubt that because of her particular style of grip, she finds it more difficult to pick up balls on the angle – although she is extremely quick – but it is her early-ball ability which helps her to be the aggressor.

Fig 30   Monica Seles, who is left-handed, playing a double-handed forehand. Note the left hand at the bottom of the racquet.

Provided that you are full of purpose, positive in the development of your own particular style, and that you really believe in what you are doing, there is room at the top for everybody.

Fig 31   Monica Seles, a prime exponent of the double-handed grip. Note how early she has taken the ball.

Fig 32   Monica Seles's facial expression reflects the aggression and effort she puts into every shot.

from the back. But times change.

As mentioned on page 35, youngsters are quite often not strong enough to cope with a single-handed grip. The natural consequence, then, is for the child to use two hands.

Only fifteen years ago this was not the norm. The advent of successful players such as Bjorn Borg, Jimmy Connors, Chris Evert and, more recently, Monica Seles – who is double-handed both sides – coupled with the fact that more people are starting to play from a young age and need support from both hands are the two main reasons behind this change.

Some schools of thought argue very strongly that we are pushing too many youngsters to take up the game too early, and that if they were encouraged to play at eleven or twelve instead, when they are more able to cope with the single-handed backhand, they could be better players.

The obvious weakness of double-handed play is the restricted reach, so please be aware that if you are going to play with two hands on the racquet, you may need extra mobility to compensate for it.

5
GRIPS – THE MECHANICS

There is no doubt that the grip you use will influence the way you shape your strokes. Despite the variety of strokes which are played, some fundamental principles will always apply. What are these basic principles?

1. Moving to and around the ball, using the small steps and body movements essential to the final adjustments to the execution of your shot.
2. Consistently getting into a good position to strike the ball.
3. Good balance and movement throughout the duration of the stroke.
4. Early preparation of the racquet.
5. Keeping in control of the racquet at all times.
6. Meeting the ball with the racquet head in front of the body.

The Eastern or Continental Grip Forehand Figs 33 and 34

Start from the ready position. On sighting the ball, make the necessary footwork and start preparing with an early takeback of the racquet. This coincides with the playing arm turning away from the ball, creating what is called a hip pivot.

On completion of the backswing, you should be aware of your weight on the back foot, ready to transfer forward in conjunction with the swinging of the racquet

Fig 33   The Eastern or Continental grip forehand – front view.

(a)   Ready position.   (b)   Early takeback.

Fig 34   The Eastern or Continental grip forehand – side view.

(a)   Early takeback.   (b)   Hip pivot – weight on the back foot.

towards The ball. As the racquet moves towards the ball, weight will be transferred from the back foot to the front foot in a stepping motion.

It is absolutely vital that you understand the value of the hip turn. I am totally against the orthodox position – that is, sideways on to the ball, before the swinging forward of the racquet – as this generally leads to loss of power.

You should be looking to strike the ball approximately level with the leading hip, at a comfortable distance from the body and at a comfortable height. Allow the racquet to fulfil the follow-through – the butt of the racquet should finish approximately head-high. The racquet head should be above the wrist during the takeback and as you follow through with the stroke, the body should finish facing the net.

(c)   Hip pivot – weight on the back foot.

(d)   Transfer your weight in conjunction with swinging the racquet towards the ball.

(e)   Follow through.

(c)   Transfer your weight in conjunction with swinging the racquet towards the ball.

(d)   Follow through.

(e)   Butt of racquet should finish approximately head-high.

The Western Grip Forehand
Fig 35

Exactly the same preparation is used as for the Eastern grip forehand. Start from the ready position. On sighting the ball, make the necessary footwork to meet the ball with an early takeback of the racquet. This coincides with the playing arm turning away from the ball, creating a hip pivot.

On completion of the backswing, you should now be aware of your weight on the back foot, ready to transfer forward in conjunction with the swinging of the racquet towards the ball.

As you start to swing the racquet forward, you will maintain an open stance, so that weight transference takes place through the strength of the legs. Again, the racquet is looking to meet the ball level with the leading hip, at a comfortable distance from the body and at a comfortable height.

Because of the Western grip, it is imperative that you use a strong wrist action through the strike zone. The follow-through should occur with a bent elbow and can often finish with the racquet facing downwards.

Be aware that on completion of the backswing, Western grip players will generally start with the racquet arm in a lower position.

Fig 35   The Western grip forehand.

(a)   Early preparation of racquet.

(b)   Hip pivot.

(c)   Strike the ball level with the leading hip.

(d)   Retain an open stance.

(e)   Follow through.

(f)   On completion of the follow-through, note the bent elbow.

Fig 36   Chris Evert – an excellent exponent of the Eastern grip forehand.

Fig 37   The single-handed backhand – front view.

(a)   Early takeback.

(b)   Note use of non-playing hand to prepare the racquet – it assists in the change of grip.

(c)   Note the shoulder turn – weight on the back foot.

(d)   Transfer your weight in conjunction with swinging the racquet towards the ball.

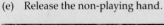

(e)   Release the non-playing hand.

(f)   Follow through.

The Single-Handed Backhand Figs 37 and 38

Once more, start from the ready position. On sighting the ball, make the necessary footwork and start preparing to meet the ball with an early takeback of the racquet. This coincides with the playing arm turning away from the ball, creating what is called a hip pivot. On completion of the backswing, you should be aware of your weight on the back foot, ready to transfer forward in conjunction with the swinging of the racquet towards the ball.

One of the advantages of the single-handed backhand is the use that can be made of the non-playing hand. The non-playing hand should be holding the racquet very lightly, and as you are making the early racquet preparation, it assists in the change of grip that is necessary for the backhand.

On completion of the backswing, you should be aware that the back of the hitting shoulder is now facing the net. As the forward swing begins, you naturally release the racquet from the non-playing hand, and to obtain maximum power the forward swing should coincide with the movement of the front foot.

Please be aware that to obtain maximum benefit from your strike, you should not go across too much with the leading leg. I would suggest striking the ball in front of the leading leg, at a comfortable distance and height from the body. The racquet will follow through with the butt again at approximately head-height.

Fig 38   The single-handed backhand – side view.

(a)   Early takeback.

(b)   Note use of non-playing hand to prepare the racquet – it assists in change of grip.

(c)   Note the shoulder turn – weight on the back foot.

(d)   Transfer your weight in conjunction with swinging the racquet towards the ball.

(e)   Release the non-playing hand.

(f)   Complete the follow-through.

47

The Double-Handed Backhand
Figs 39 and 40

Again, start from the ready position. On sighting the ball, make the necessary footwork, and start preparing to meet the ball with an early takeback of the racquet. This coincides with the playing arm turning away from the ball, creating what is called the hip pivot. On completion of the backswing, you should now be aware of your weight on the back foot, ready to transfer forward in conjunction with the swinging of the racquet towards the ball.

Two areas that require specific attention for the double-handed player are:

1. You must get closer to the ball because of the restriction caused by having two hands on the racquet.
2. Because of the need for both hands to be brought on together for harmony within the stroke, early preparation is imperative.

Once again, when transferring the backswing to the forward swing, be aware of the weight transfer from the back to the front foot. You should be looking to strike the ball out in front of the leading hip.

There are two ways of completing the double-handed stroke. One is by retaining both hands on the racquet and following through across the shoulder, and the other is by releasing the top hand and completing with an orthodox follow-through (see Fig 40).

Fig 39   The double-handed backhand.

(a)   Early takeback coincides with the hip pivot – weight on the back foot.

(b)   Note closeness of the ball to the body because of the restriction caused by having two hands on the racquet.

Fig 40   The double-handed backhand – with release.

(a)   Early takeback.

(b)   Note closeness of the ball to the body because of the restriction caused by having two hands on the racquet.

(c)   Transfer your weight in conjunction with swinging the racquet towards the ball.

(d)   Retain both hands on the racquet.

(e)   Follow through across the shoulder.

(c)   Strike the ball in front of the leading hip.

(d)   Release the top hand.

(e)   Full follow-through.

Fig 41   The forehand volley.

(a)   Ready position.

(b)   Hip pivot and short takeback.

(c)   Keep the racquet head above the wrist.

The Volley
Figs 41 and 42

Obviously, because you are playing close to the net, there is much less time available to prepare for the shot.

As already discussed in Chapter 4, to be a successful net player the use of one grip, the chopper grip, is essential. However, if you are a beginner and feel more comfortable in the early stages using the conventional forehand and backhand grips, please do so – but remember that if you really do wish to improve your volleying prowess, the less grip change you eventually have to make, the better.

We shall embrace both the forehand (*see* Fig 41) and backhand volleys (*see* Fig 42) together for the purpose of this explanation.

It is important when learning the mechanics of the volley to understand that the volley stroke is a very short and simple action.

Start in the normal ready

(d)   Transfer the weight in conjunction with a simple punching motion.

(e)   Keep the follow-through to a minimum.

position, but hold the racquet higher than you would do for groundstokes.

On sighting the ball, the feet will move into position to execute the shot. Again, it is vital to emphasize the importance of a good hip pivot

position as you prepare the racquet for the shot. Because of the shortness of the stroke I would suggest you take the racquet no further back than a forty-five degree turn of the shoulder from the ready position.

Fig 42   The backhand volley.

(a)   Ready position.

(b)   Hip pivot.

(c)   Short takeback.

(d)   Weight on the back foot.

(e)   Weight transference.

(f)   Simple punching motion.

Once again, coincide the weight transference with the forward motion of the racquet by stepping forward with the front foot. You are seeking to play the ball slightly in front of the body with a blocking or punching motion.

Be aware that a firm wrist at impact is required and that you must try to keep the follow-through down to a minimum. Be aware also that upon execution of the shot a quick recovery will be necessary, so as to play the next shot.

Fig 43   The serve – side view.

(a)   Ready position.

(b)   Fix the eyes at the target – weight on the back foot.

(c)   . . . slots into the 'backscratch' position . . .

(e)   . . . where the racquet goes over the shoulder and appears to drop down towards the shoulder blade.

(f)   Raise the elbow to approximately shoulder-height.

(g)   Note the extension of the arm at impact.

(d) Place the ball in the air as the racquet swings back in a pendulum motion .

(h)   Follow through.

The Serve
Figs 43 and 44

The value of a good service goes without saying. The service starts play-off and developing a fine serve is crucial to your game as a whole.

Some players have achieved a high status within the game mainly by virtue of their excellent serve, so it is worth finding the time to put in extra effort to achieve a sound service action.

Service styles vary greatly but certain basics will always apply. What you are looking for in the service action is a simple technique which allows the racquet to gather momentum as it is thrown at the ball. The key to producing a fine serve lies in this throwing action.

And now to the mechanics. Assume the ready position: stand behind the baseline in a sideways position, similar to the one you would use for throwing a ball. To achieve good co-ordination between the ball and racquet hand, I would suggest starting with the ball held against the strings of the racquet or at the throat of the racquet. Then, fix the eyes at the target. When you feel ready to start the action, allow the racquet to swing back in a pendulum motion, past the back leg, to finally slot into the classic position called 'backscratch', where the racquet goes over the shoulder and appears to drop down and touch the shoulder blade. This action encourages the elbow to be raised to approximately shoulder-height.

As this procedure is going on, two other events should be occurring. There should be a natural transference of weight onto the back foot and, just as the racquet is passing the back leg, the ball hand should begin its movement to place the ball in the air.

When placing the ball in the air, you should try to visualize placing it at a comfortable full hitting height, as well as comfortably in front of the body.

At this stage, the racquet head momentum should be increasing from the backscratch position before being thrown aggressively at the ball. At the same time, you should be stretching the arm upwards to acquire the maximum hitting height.

In an ideal service action, extra power is sought by what is called wrist snap, used just prior to impact. The racquet, after striking the ball, will then follow through across the body and past the forward leg. One extra tip: the racquet should not be held in a strangle-hold. It should be held as lightly as possible, without losing control, as this undoubtedly encourages greater head speed.

We have just discussed the classic style of serve. Be aware that other styles exist. All of them, however, will be following a co-ordinated method, so that optimum racquet-head speed is produced.

Take Roscoe Tanner, for example, a journeyman player of the late seventies. He manages a fast service action with a comparatively low ball toss. Then there are Roger Taylor (former British Davis Cup player) and Pam Shriver, who do not use the natural co-ordination between the two hands at the outset of the action.

53

Fig 44   The serve – front view.

(a)   Ready position.

(b)   Fix the eyes at the target.

(c)   Weight on the back foot.

(e)   . . . slots into the 'backscratch' position . . .

(f)   . . . where the racquet goes over the shoulder and appears to drop down and touch the shoulder blade. Raise the elbow to approximately shoulder-height.

(g)   Fully extend the arm.

(d)   Place the ball in the air as the racquet swings back in a pendulum motion . . .

(h)   Follow through.

Fig 45   Edberg here displays all the attributes of a great server.

The Smash
Fig 46

The one fundamental principle of the smash is exactly the same as that of the serve: you are seeking to get the racquet into the backscratch position, in order to generate as much controlled power as possible through a throwing action.

One of the greatest rewards of achieving a good overhead shot is the superb feeling you receive from smashing the ball away, and if you are to develop security at the net, you will have to develop a fine smash to complement the volleys.

The mechanics are as follows. Stand in the ready position, as for volleying. On sighting the lob, your first move should be to turn the racquet shoulder away from the net whilst taking a large stride back with the back foot to achieve a very mobile position. You are now in the ideal position to make the required movements and adjustments that are vital to an effective smash. As you are

Fig 46   The smash.

(a)   Ready position.

(b)   Fix the eyes at the target.

(c)   Sideways-on position, short takeback, pointing with left hand.

(d)   'Backscratch' position.

(e)   Fully extend the arm.

(f)   Follow through across the leading leg.

56

performing the first move, take the racquet back into the backscratch position. Some players use a method similar to the service action, but the majority take the racquet back with a much shorter backswing, almost taking the racquet across their face.

Having achieved the backscratch position, follow the same mechanics as in the serve.

The major difference between the serve and the smash is the obvious fact that the ball has been placed in the air by your opponent and, naturally, he is trying to put the ball in the most awkward place he can.

So, with the smash, you are confronted with a moving ball situation; that is why your first movement is so important, and you should move into a sideways-on position as efficiently and quickly as you can. You will always struggle to smash well if you move back on your heels. Use the non-playing hand as a sighting for the ball by pointing toward it.

Always be aware when using the smash that you are in control of the situation, and even if your first smash has not won you the point, it will be setting you up for the kill on the next shot. Over the years I

Fig 47 Martina is showing excellent improvisation with a ball that is too close to her body.

have been astounded by the number of good players who hit the ball into the net because they are over-anxious to finish off the point.

The Lob
Figs 48 and 49

For the moment, we will look at the basic lob. The lob is used in trying to keep your opponent away from the net and, in most instances, it tends to be used as a last resort when the passing shot is not producing results.

The most important factor in good lobbing is to use the same preparation as you would for a normal groundstroke, whether forehand or backhand. Having followed the normal prep-aration, just as the forward swing is starting to take effect, the racquet will drop into a lower position, to create the right angle of an open racquet face needed at impact. Once you have created the low racquet position, lift the racquet in a steep upward motion, from low to high, continuing through so that the racquet is pointing to the sky.

Disguise is important for success and will be discussed in Chapter 10.

Fig 48   The forehand lob.

(a)   Prepare as for a forehand groundstroke.

(b)   Weight on the back foot, ready to drop the racquet into a low position.

Fig 49   The backhand lob.

(a)   Prepare as for a backhand groundstroke.

(b)   Takeback – weight on the back foot . . .

(c)   . . . ready to drop the racquet into a lower position.

(c)   Note the open racquet face.

(d)   Lift the racquet in an upward motion – note how the ball rises steeply off the strings.

(e)   Follow through with the racquet pointing to the sky.

(d)   Note the open racquet face.

(e)   Lift the racquet in an upward motion.

(f)   Follow through with the racquet pointing to the sky.

59

6

SPINS

Now that you have been given an insight into the basic strokes that will allow you to venture onto a tennis court, let us now move on to a new area; one which I personally regard as the most enjoyable part of the game. That is, learning how to change the flight, speed and variety of shots by using various spins (*see* Fig 50).

There are essentially three different ways to hit a tennis ball. One is to hit it flat, which will always carry a very small element of sidespin for control. The second one is with slice, which will also carry an element of sidespin, and the third is with topspin, (*see* Fig 51).

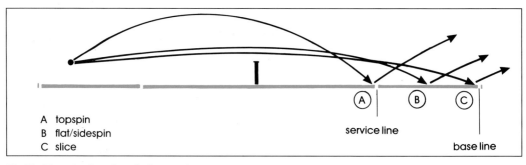

A topspin
B flat/sidespin
C slice

service line

base line

Fig 50 Topspin, flat, slice (flight over the net).

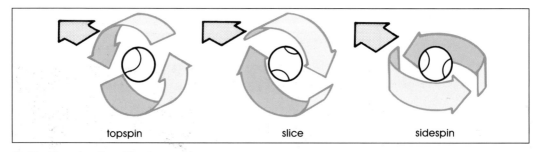

topspin   slice   sidespin

Fig 51 Topspin, slice, sidespin.

When first learning to play, the orthodox strokes encourage you to hit the ball flat, but certain degrees of spin are generally applied subconsciously for control purposes.

Spin is used for two reasons:

1. To obtain greater control of the ball.

2. To use it tactically to upset the opposition's rhythm.

It is worth mentioning that within the game today, players who achieve success merely by hitting flat or lifted ground-strokes have become obsolete. One obvious exception is Jimmy Connors, but he may well be the last of his kind.

There is a tendency among the women players, particularly the Americans such as Jennifer Capriati and Chris Evert, to base their game around the lifted groundstroke. But it is worth emphasizing that both parties hit the ball with more sidespin or topspin than the normal eye can detect.

Fig 52

The main danger associated with striking the ball flat is that the margin for error is very low. Because of the very nature of the flat strike, the ball will be struck hard, and therefore to keep the ball within the playing area it will also have an extremely low flight. Hence the difficulty of playing error-free tennis with such a method.

Common sense therefore dictates that, to keep the margin of error to a minimum, you must hit the ball higher over the net – this is where topspin has a role – and if you wish to maintain a low flight over the net, you must use slice and sidespin for control.

Topspin

So, how can you obtain topspin?

Topspin is achieved by brushing up the back of the ball with a closed racquet face. This causes the ball to rotate with a controlled overspin action. Once you have created the topspin, the ball in flight will rotate away from you.

The use of topspin promotes a safer margin of error when the ball is clearing the net, and you can safely use a net clearance of 1.5 or 1.8m (5 or 6ft) when you are rallying with this spin.

Upon striking the court surface, the ball will travel forward with a high bounce, which makes it difficult for your opponent to retrieve (*see* below).

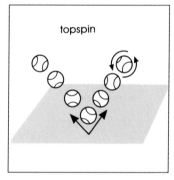

Fig 53 Ball bouncing off the court with topspin. High (steep) approach angle and bounce.

Fig 54 Jennifer Capriati imparting topspin off her forehand.

Fig 55 Steffi Graf is renowned for her forehand, but she also has a sound and efficient sliced backhand.

Slice and Sidespin

The second method of spin actually incorporates two complementary spins: slice and side. It will be almost impossible to produce one without the other.

Slice

When imparting slice, you will be striking the ball with the racquet face open and sliding under the ball, and the motion of the follow-through gives the ball its forward momentum. The ball travels slowly through the air, because this time it is revolving back towards you.

Sidespin

Sidespin is self-explanatory. When making the sliced shot,

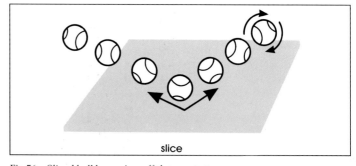

Fig 56 Sliced ball bouncing off the court at a low angle.

you will be striking the ball on its side to a certain degree, and the element of sidespin this creates will affect the amount of movement the ball will make when it strikes the playing surface.

The two assets of playing with slice and sidespin are:

1. Because the ball is travelling more slowly, you can play with a lower margin of error, keeping the ball as low as 15cm (6in) over the net.
2. On making contact with the ground, the ball will keep lower thanks to the slicing effect, as shown above.

7
SPINS – THE MECHANICS

In order to incorporate the spins into the way you play, you will obviously have to adapt the mechanics you already possess to obtain full benefit from the spin. Be it forehand or backhand, the same basic skills will apply.

Topspin

There are two ways of producing topspin. One is by using the big shoulder muscles (this is what I call the arm topspin), and the other is by using the smaller muscles – the forearm and the wrist.

Very rarely will you see players, when they are swapping groundstrokes from the baseline, hit winners with their topspin. In that particular predicament, it is the mental ability to keep a consistent, error-free rhythm which eventually pays dividends. The object here is to wear the opponent down.

However, to be successful on the Men's Tour today, topspin should be an almost obligatory part of your armoury. This is also beginning to be the case on the Women's Tour, as they become stronger and more adept at using topspin. Players who are using topspin effectively include Gabriela Sabatini – who uses it on both wings – and Steffi Graf – who has a very aggressive topspin forehand.

Players who are using topspin so successfully do not only rally well with this method, but they also prove

Fig 57   Here is a typical Sabatini forehand follow-through.

very difficult to attack for two reasons:

1.   It is very difficult to attack groundstrokes that carry so much topspin.
2.   Topspin is a very effective means of playing passing shots if your opponent is seeking to go to the net.

There is no doubt that players who like to attack the net are very respectful of any opponents who use topspin, because they find themselves frequently confused by the amount of topspin imparted upon the ball.

The element of surprise can be extremely effective.

Topspin Groundstrokes

As discussed earlier, the grip you use will determine your style of play, so it will be almost inevitable that if you use the Western or Semi-Western grip, your strokes will be based around topspin. You really have very little choice of playing any other way, while the Eastern or Continental players, by virtue of their grip, will have more flexibility in their choice of spins.

I can assure you that topspin is possible even if you are a Continental-grip player – Rod Laver is a perfect example (*see* page 61). However, to play a topspin forehand with the Continental grip does require very strong forearms and wrists.

We have already agreed that imparting topspin requires a brushing motion of the racquet face up and over the ball. Therefore, to be a successful topspin player you should prepare for a topspin groundstroke with a looping action. This will create the right shape and momentum to produce the topspin required.

The same fundamental principles as for the basic groundstrokes will apply (*see* Chapter 5). You need good footwork, early preparation of the racquet, and a good hip turn to create the pivot which is so essential to obtain weight transference. But this is where the stroke differs.

As you feel you are about to transfer your weight forward into the strike, the racquet

head will drop into a lower position, allowing you to swing the racquet with an aggressive upward motion against the back of the ball at impact (*see* Figs 60 and 61). According to the degree of topspin required, you can use your wrist action to encourage greater head speed; almost like whipping at the ball.

In order to execute a successful topspin forehand, you should maintain an open stance (i.e. throughout the duration of the stroke, your feet remain approximateely square to the net). This encourages you to use the body weight as part of the whipping action. (In fact, it is a common characteristic for topspin groundstroke players to become airborne when playing their shot.)

Fig 58   Capriati illustrates the dropped racquet head and open stance needed to produce topspin.

Fig 59   Jennifer Capriati follows through from an open-stance forehand.

Fig 60   The topspin forehand.

(a)   Takeback.

(b)   Weight on the back foot.

(c)   Drop the racquet into a lower position.

(d)   Transfer your weight in conjunction with swinging the racquet towards the ball.

(e)   Open stance – created because of the aggressive upward motion.

(f)   Follow through – the racquet head flips over and points to the ground.

Because of the momentum and aggressiveness of the stroke, the follow-through can vary between finishing high above your head or with the racquet head flipping over so that the racquet face points to the ground. A prime exponent of this latter finish is Steffi Graf.

Topspin can therefore be interpreted in a variety of ways and styles. Two-handed players can also use topspin as part of their repertoire, following the same principles as those just discussed, within the framework of their own mechanics. They have an advantage in that being so much closer to the ball, they are able to produce finer angles on some of their shots.

Fig 61   The topspin backhand.

(a)   Takeback – weight on the back foot.

(b)   Drop the racquet into a lower position.

(c)   Transfer your weight in conjunction with swinging the racquet towards the ball.

(d)   Follow through.

(e)   The racquet head flips over . . .

(f)   . . . and points to the ground.

Fig 64

Figs 62, 63 and 64   Three different examples of the open-stance forehand.

Fig 63

The Sliced Sidespin

Unlike topspin, which only recently became a feature of most players' repertoire, slice has always been part of the game.

It has always been effective within the game, predominantly because it remains a very useful defensive shot. It is a simple stroke to produce, and is at its most beneficial when your opponent is applying pressure.

Simplicity and economy of effort will allow you to be effective with this stroke while under pressure. This pressure can be applied by the weight of shot, or by the variation and placement of the ball.

Using slice is the most effective way of gaining accurate placement of the ball and this creates the opportunity to change the pace and length of the rally and can therefore upset your opponent's game.

Because slice keeps the ball low to the ground after striking the surface, it can be used to good effect against opponents

67

who are reluctant to get down to the low ball and it can also be used as a deterrent against topspinners who find it difficult to produce their topspin off very low-bouncing balls. It is also a valuable shot when you are seeking to approach the net – this will be discussed in-depth in Chapter 9, page 98.

Slice has always been used by fine clay court and grass court players, because of the very nature of those surfaces. Both grass and clay are very receptive to the sliced ball, hence the value of adding this shot to your game. Many great players use slice effectively in their game, and two obvious examples are Martina Navratilova and John McEnroe.

Before we take a closer look at the mechanics of the shot, one of the weaknesses of the Western grip must be mentioned, and that is the difficulty it creates in playing a sliced forehand. While discussing the mechanics of the sliced groundstrokes, it will be on the assumption that you are playing with an Eastern or Continental grip.

Very few players will use the sliced forehand as a standard stroke (Pam Shriver is one exception), whereas on the backhand wing, slice can be the mainstay. Both Steffi Graf and Martina Navratilova are excellent exponents of this.

The sliced forehand (see Fig 65) is far more difficult to play than the sliced backhand (see Fig 66), which probably explains why so few players use it as their main stroke.

Preparation for a sliced groundstroke will, as always, require good footwork to get into position and execute the shot. The best method of taking the racquet back is either a straight takeback (commonly used by American players), or a very shallow loop. Raise the racquet head upon completion of the backswing above the height at which you are intending to strike the ball. As before, it is important that your weight be on the back foot with a sound hip turn. On the forehand side, you will be seeking to strike the ball at the side of your body, whereas on the backhand side, the ball will be slightly in front.

On completion of the backswing, not only will the racquet be held higher, but the racquet face will be slightly open. As you swing and transfer your weight forward, be aware that your racquet will travel from above to below the ball, striking the back of the ball firmly through the impact zone.

It is vital on this particular shot that you transfer your weight by stepping into the shot. This weight transference really will add extra bite to your backspin. As you slide the racquet face under the ball, you should really seek out the sensation that you are holding the ball on the racquet face for a long period.

Two types of follow-through can be used. One is very similar to a chopping action when the racquet head virtually stops at impact; the other is when you allow the racquet to flow through to eventually achieve an approximate head-height position.

Fig 65 The sliced forehand.

(a)   High takeback.

(b)   Slightly open racquet face.

(c)   Strike the ball at the side of the body.

(d)   Slide the racquet face under the ball – note the open racquet face.

(e)   Follow through.

(f)   Short follow-through on completion of the stroke.

Fig 66   The sliced backhand.

(a)   Early preparation.

(b)   Hip pivot.

(c)   High takeback.

(d)   Strike the ball at the side of the body.

(e)   Step into the shot.

(f)   Follow through to approximately head-height.

The Double-Handed Slice

This is an area which over the years has caused double-handed players some problems. They really do look very uncomfortable playing this shot. The top hand does not allow for the fluidity required to play the shot soundly. On the whole, double-handed players use it as a last resort – as a defence from the back of the court. It is fairly common practice, under extreme pressure, for double-handed players to play single-handed sliced backhands.

The double-handed slice is a shot which Mats Wilander has cultivated, to such an extent that he has almost become single-handed whilst playing a sliced backhand.

Fig 67   Stefan Edberg prepares to play an exemplary sliced backhand.

Fig 68   The topspin forehand lob.

(a)   Prepare as for a normal stroke.

(b)   Takeback. Drop the racquet to a lower position.

(c)   Strike the ball at the side of the body.

Fig 69   The topspin backhand lob.

(a)   Takeback.

(b)   Drop the racquet to a lower position.

(c)   Strike the ball at the side of the body – keep an open stance.

(d)   Use an aggressive writst action at impact, brushing up and over the ball.

(e)   High follow-through.

(d)   Use an aggressive wrist action at impact, brushing up and over the ball.

(e)   High follow-through.

The Topspin Lob
Figs 68 and 69

It is hard to believe that until recent times this shot was something of a rarity, whereas today it is part of all good players' game.

The topspin lob is a must if you want to keep a good net player at bay. It is probably the shot that net players fear most. When the lob has been successfully played, it is almost impossible to run the ball down because the topspin causes the ball to accelerate off the court.

Another advantage of possessing a topsin lob is that the net player will instinctively hold back from his normal attacking position to guard against the lob. This, naturally, will give the groundstroker more time and space to play his passing shots.

The value of the lob is therefore twofold and you can see why it has now achieved such a prominent position in the groundstroke player's repertoire of shots.

It is far easier to play a topspin lob off the forehand side than it is off the backhand, as the aggressive wrist action that is required to play the shot lends itself to the forehand side. To be able to play a backhand topspin lob, you must have an extremely strong forehand and wrist. The best exponent of this is probably Ivan Lendl.

The more extreme the forehand and backhand grips are, the easier it will be to obtain the aggressive wrist action required for a truly effective lob. The better you can disguise your preparation for that shot, the greater the effect in surprising the opposition.

Now to the mechanics (see Figs 68 and 69).

In preparing for the shot, try to create as orthodox a backswing as you can.

Delay as long as possible the change from backswing to forward swing. In all probability, because of the delay, you will be playing the shot at the side of your body, necessitating a very open stance as the ball drops lower than normal.

When the time is right to transfer your weight into the strike, drop the racquet head quickly into a very low position to attack the ball with an aggressive wrist action, brushing up and over the ball in the same motion. This, linked with a body action that levers itself off the ground through a very powerful leg action, will promote the vicious topspin that you are seeking.

This aggressive action results in a very high follow-through, finishing with the racquet well above your head.

Double-handed players are very adept at this shot. They have an ability to delay it longer than single-handers because the top hand can give them that little extra whip into the shot.

The Sliced Lob

People tend to assume that the sliced lob is a defensive shot. However, it can be cultivated into an extremely efficient attacking shot, if played wisely and at the right time.

The key to this shot is for you to be aware that the net player is committed to moving forward from his previous shot and you therefore play the lob with a much lower flight than when playing the defensive lob. You can almost call it a 'sharp, shallow lob'.

Two players who use this shot to perfection are Miloslav Mecir and Chris Evert. It is interesting to note that they are both double-handers.

The mechanics are almost identical to those of the defensive lob. What varies is the position from which you play the shot.

The defensive lob is generally played from behind the baseline when there is no alternative but to try and get yourself back in the rally with a very high lob, whereas the 'sharp, shallow lob' is played when you have a choice of shot and you are in a control position. The difference is that you will be attempting an attacking sliced lob, and at the moment of impact you attack the ball with a sharp, firm, open racquet face. The follow-through will be infinitely shorter than when playing the defensive lob.

Fig 70   Throughout her long and illustrious career Chris Evert used the lob to devastating effect.

Spin on Serve

For many people this is an Achilles' heel. The reason for this is that they find the chopper grip extremely uncomfortable to use.

So far, I have advocated freedom of choice as far as grips are concerned. However, in order to develop the necessary variation of spins with the service action, the chopper grip is absolutely vital. Do not be fooled by Boris Becker. He is one in a million. (*See* page 38).

I have had many pupils come to me with a very able first serve – achieved on the strength of the dreaded 'frying pan' grip – who then plead for a second serve. You simply cannot achieve the wrist flexibility necessary to produce spin with the 'frying pan' grip. There is no alternative but to use the chopper grip.

The immediate ordeal involved in changing to the chopper grip will pay long term dividends. The main bonus will be greater confidence in your entire game.

You will be able to use a very aggressive first serve, confident in the knowledge that your second serve is more secure. By using spin on your serve, you will also keep your opponent guessing as to what serve he is about to receive. This will give you a psychological advantage when serving.

You will naturally be using your spin from above your head and will be making contact with the ball in a different area, but the sooner you are prepared to experiment, the sooner will you feel at ease in this area.

The Topspin Serve
Figs 72 and 73

The best asset of the topspin

Fig 71   Stefan Edberg's topspin serve is feared on the Men's Tour.

server is that he creates greater net clearance, and therefore the margin for error is increased. Because the ball has a higher trajectory over the net, you will have more time to get into position for the next shot. This can be particularly rewarding if you wish to play a volley behind your serve, and this is why the topspin serve is used so effectively in doubles. It will also cause problems for the opponent because of its unpredictability. On contact with the playing surface, the ball will bounce higher and sharper than a normal flat serve.

Producing a successful topspin serve requires aggression, which is psychologically beneficial because you are less likely to feel nervous when attacking a ball.

The topspin serve is likely to cause more problems to a groundstroker's backhand than to the forehand, as it is more difficult to play backhands with a high bouncing ball.

Certain surfaces, such as clay courts or cement, will take the effect of topspin better than others (*see* Chapter 27).

Let us now look at the mechanics The key to the success of the topspin serve is the placement of the ball. You will not be able to complete a successful serve unless the ball is placed correctly.

The preparation is similar to that used for the flat serve. As you prepare for the serve, arch the back, as this will encourage the ball to be positioned slightly behind the ball-placing shoulder at the climax of the toss. It is the combination of the back arch and different ball placement which enables the server to attack the ball with a very wristy throwing action, taking the racquet face up and over the back of the ball (*see* below).

Be aware that the brushing action of the racquet face is absolutely essential to obtain the required topspin. The follow-through of the racquet is much more up and out than with the flat serve and will result in the racquet finishing almost against the back leg.

Fig 72   Topspin serve brushing over the ball.

Fig 73   The topspin serve.

(a)   Preparation for the serve.

(b)   Keep the knees bent . . .

(f)   Use elevation for extra power.

(g)   Brush the racquet face up and over the back of the ball.

(c) . . . and the back arched . . .

(d) . . . so that the ball is positioned slightly behind the ball-placing shoulder, . . .

(e) . . . giving the aggressive power needed for the topspin.

(h) Follow through.

(i) Follow through up and out . . .

(j) . . . finishing almost against the back leg.

Use your legs as much as possible for the topspin serve: the more you can bend your knees and link this action to the back arch, the greater topspin will you be able to produce.

The Kick Serve

This is a slight variation on the topspin serve. The big difference between these two serves is that to get the extra 'kick' into the action a greater knee bend is required – since much of the power is created from the strength of your legs. Again, Boris Becker really does reflect this perfectly.

The Sliced Serve
Figs 74, 75 and 76

There is always a small amount of slice on a flat serve for control purposes. The sliced serve does not carry the safety margin of the topspin serve, but nevertheless it still presents a variation for the second serve.

Because of the variation in speed and flight of the ball, linked to a bounce that swerves away from, or into, the opponent, the sliced serve is valuable as an alternative second serve, as it keeps your opponent guessing. As the ball swerves through the air and off the court surface, it can create problems for your opponent by taking him out of the court. The sliced serve also cuts into your opponent's body region, so restricting his hitting area.

Not only is the slice a good alternative for a second serve, but it can also be used very effectively as a first serve weapon, in particular on grass courts and other low-bouncing surfaces.

Prepare as normal (see Fig 75). Again, the key to producing a good sliced serve is in the placement of the ball. You will be seeking to place the ball slightly lower than normal and to the side, away from the body.

Use a strong throwing action with the racquet face semi-closed at impact, and as the racquet follows through, try to create a strong cutting motion around the outside of the ball (see Fig 74). Imagine that the ball is staying on the strings for as long as possible.

With a good sliced serve, the follow-through will go well across the body on completion of the stroke.

When you begin to throw the racquet out of the back-scratch position towards the ball, be aware that because the ball has been placed lower than normal the speed of the racquet should be quicker than normal (see Fig 76).

Fig 74   Sliced serve cutting around the outside of the ball.

Fig 75   The sliced serve.

(a)   Preparation for the serve.

(e)   . . . and to the side, away from the body.

(b)   Weight on the
back foot.

(c)   Place the ball in the
air . . .

(d)   . . . slightly lower
than normal . . .

(f)   Keep the racquet face
semi-closed at impact.

(g)   Create a strong
cutting motion around the outside
of the ball.

(h)   Follow through across the
body.

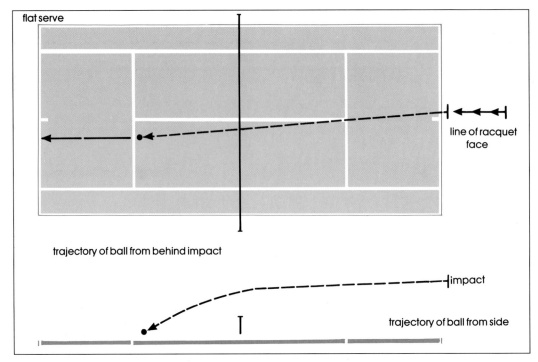

flat serve

trajectory of ball from behind impact

line of racquet face

impact

trajectory of ball from side

Figs 76 (a)–(c)   Flight paths of the different types of serve – reaction of the ball off the court.

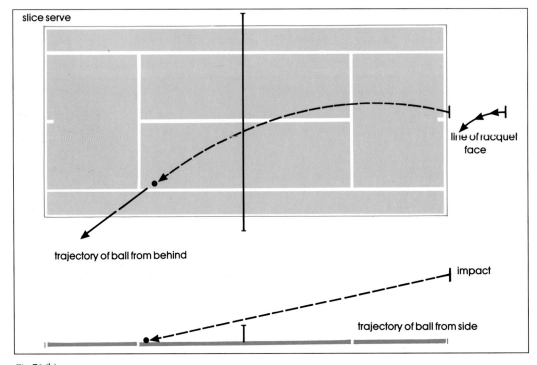

slice serve

trajectory of ball from behind

line of racquet face

impact

trajectory of ball from side

Fig 76 (b)

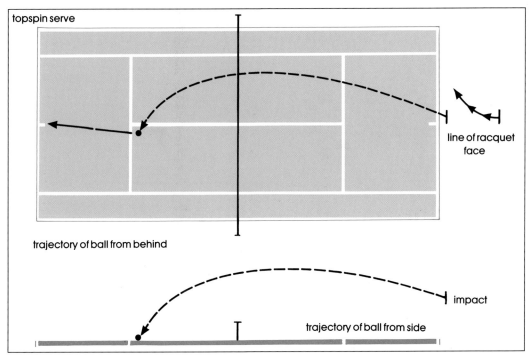

topspin serve

line of racquet face

trajectory of ball from behind

impact

trajectory of ball from side

Fig 76 (c)

Spin on Smash

The Topspin Smash

This will probably be used under three circumstances:

1.   For variation.
2.   When the lob is very high and you choose to let it bounce, and the ball bounces high enough to be converted into a smash.
3.   When your opponent has tried to lob you over your backhand side.

Seeking to play a smash in all these situations will assist you in retaining the attacking position.

Combine the technique of the orthodox smash with the concepts of the topspin serve. However, you will probably have to jump to play this shot and the need for the back arch is absolutely vital.

The Sliced Smash

This will be used under the following circumstances:

1.   For variation.
2.   When the ball is not quite high enough to make an orthodox smash, but you can move your feet into position to impart slice on the overhead.
3.   When a sliced smash will enable you to create an angle when killing the ball.
4.   When the lob is extremely deep you can allow the ball to bounce, and as the ball reaches a height suitable for smashing, you can play a smash which enables you to retain the attacking role.

Apply the same mechanics as for an orthodox smash, but make the necessary adjustments, as if you were imparting slice on the serve.

8
THE IMPROVISED SHOTS

Tennis is not just about basic strokes. As you become involved in the game you will experience situations where the basic shots simply are not enough. Sometimes during match play – either because your opponent is forcing you into difficult situations or because there is a need to change tactics – you will be required to play an improvised shot.

In this category are the following shots: the half volley, the drop shot, the drop volley, the drive volley, the lob volley, the low volley, the dink, the under-arm serve, the backhand smash and the round arm smash.

The Half Volley
Fig 77

When first learning to play the game, a large number of people are led to think that the half volley is to be avoided at all costs.

Personally, I believe this to be an error, because when used with understanding, the half volley is a very valuable shot – one great exponent being Monica Seles, who appears to half volley a high percentage of her groundstrokes.

The shot is generally used in one of two situations:

1. At the back of the court, when the pressure created by the opponent is simply too great to allow you to move into the orthodox position.
2. When you are in the vicinity of the net but unable to make the proper volleying position.

Although the shot is called a half volley, it is technically a groundstroke. The racquet literally plays the ball just after it has struck the playing surface.

One of the benefits of the half volley is that it maintains your position on the court. This is extremely useful when you are playing at the net as it will possibly enable you to maintain pressure on your opponent. It also helps you to

Fig 77   The half volley.

(a)   Short takeback.

(b)   Pick up the ball straight after the bounce, get down low to the ball.

(c)   Strike the ball in front of the body.

recover from difficult situations.

Because there is so little time when you half volley, there will be very little backswing involved.

It is advisable to half volley with the ball well in front of the body and it is vital to get down low to the shot by bending the knees well. The racquet head at impact will be very close to the ground.

As you follow through, you should really try to carry the ball on the strings of the racquet and use some leverage from your legs to help elevate the ball over the net (*see* Fig 77(e)).

The Drop Shot
Fig 78

The drop shot must be part of your repertoire of shots if you have any desire to become a successful singles player. It is used most frequently on the slow surfaces, such as clay, and is an extremely important asset when playing an opponent who has a very secure backcourt game.

The drop shot takes pace off the ball and changes the momentum of the opposition's attack. Playing such a delicate shot breaks up your opponent's rhythm and security. It is obviously useful against a slow-moving player and can be used to draw a poor volleyer to the net position.

If used wisely, it can pay dividends, but you should never think of the drop shot as a winning shot. If you are going to play tennis at an advanced level, the probability is that the opposition will anticipate the shot and consequently retrieve the ball and keep it in play. Therefore, the back-up shot to the drop shot is equally important, as that is generally the one that will finalize the rally and win you the point. If the drop shot ends up being a winner, that is a bonus. However, you must expect the opposition to chase the ball and make the play. Be aware that it is setting you up for your next shot, which will be the lob or the pass.

The further away from the net you are, the more difficult it will be to play the shot.

Disguising the drop shot can be the key to success. It is easier to disguise the shot off the backhand than off the forehand, as the normal shape of a forehand does not easily lend itself to producing the backspin needed for this shot.

To play the drop shot, (*see* Fig 78) you prepare as you would for an orthodox groundstroke, delaying as long as possible the forward motion of the stroke.

On producing the forward swing, the racquet face will have to become open to the ball. Slide the racquet underneath the ball to create the appropriate angle needed to give the backspin that is necessary for success.

(d)   Carry the ball on the strings.

(e)   Use leverage from the legs . . .

(f)   . . . to elevate the ball over the net.

Fig 78 The forehand drop shot.

(a) Open racquet face.

(b) Keep the racquet face open.

(c) Slide the racquet underneath the ball.

(d) Extend the follow-through to approximately waist-height.

At this point, the weight is transferring forward through the legs and the follow-through of the racquet is extended to approximately waist-height.

One of the arts of playing this shot lies in the ability to absorb the pace that is coming to you and then, within the production of the stroke, to soften the ball. This is a very personalized shot, and with experience and experimentation, the shot will come naturally.

The Drop Volley
Figs 79 and 80

If you want to develop your game around the net, the drop volley (or the stop volley as it can sometimes be called) is a must. Although it requires a delicate touch, it is used as a means of attack and to change the pattern of play. There are two major opportunities for using the drop volley:

1. When you create an attack which causes your opponent to defend behind the baseline. This gives you the opportunity to play the drop volley as a winning shot.
2. When your opponent is slow to advance up the court, you can use it to place him in an awkward position in which to play his next shot.

The mechanics are very similar to those of the drop shot, but the obvious difference is that you are taking the ball out of the air.

Use the same preparation as for a normal volley, again emphasizing the delay in the production of the shot for a better disguise. This is of paramount importance if the shot is to be successful. I would suggest using a shorter backswing than normal.

As you start the execution of the shot, open the racquet face, as this will give you the angle for the required stroke. Then, allow the racquet to slide under the ball. The more aggressive you are with this action the more backspin will you create.

It is important to experiment with this sensitive shot in order to gain the confidence necessary to use it success-fully. The stop volley is played most effectively when the ball is at net-height or below.

Fig 79   The forehand drop volley.

(a)   Prepare as for a normal stroke.

(b)   Keep the racquet face open.

(c)   Slide the racquet underneath the ball . . .

(d)   . . . in a cutting motion.

(e)   Extend the follow-through . . .

(f)   . . . to approximately waist-height.

Fig 80   The backhand drop volley.

(a)   Prepare as for a normal stroke.

(b)   Keep the racquet face open.

(c)   Slide the racquet underneath the ball.

(d)   Extend the follow-through to appoximately waist-height.

Fig 81   Notice the use of the non-playing hand which gives Edberg balance when playing the drop shot.

Please be aware that you will need to experiment and practise a lot to get the full benefit of the drop volley and the drop shot. I would suggest that you use them sparingly, so retaining an element of surprise. Realize too that the surface will dictate whether and how much these shots are used.

The Drive Volley
Figs 82 and 83

The drive volley is rarely used, but when it is, the aggressive execution of the shot means that the point is usually won or lost instantly.

The drive volley is generally played from the midcourt zone, when the ball is travelling slowly through the air at about shoulder-height. The same technique as for a high forehand or backhand groundstroke is used and, usually, an element of topspin is required to keep the ball in play.

It can also be used tactically when you are playing against a dour groundstroker who could be using the 'moonball' method against you, that is, he could in effect be playing the lob shot when both of you are actually standing on the baseline. To break up the monotony, you can advance from behind the baseline and use the drive volley.

Because of the extreme difficulty involved in playing this particular shot, you will very rarely see single-handed backhand players attempt it. It really is best used on the forehand side, or by double-handed players who will obviously impart that extra strength.

This shot is for the more adventurous players and no one performs it better than Monica Seles.

Fig 82   The forehand drive volley.

(a)   Keep the feet moving to launch into the shot.

(b)   Full backswing – take the ball well above net-height . . .

Fig 83   The backhand drive volley.

(a)   Keep the feet moving to launch into the shot.

(b)   Full backswing – take the ball well above net-height . . .

The drive volley requires a very full backswing and as you start to prepare for the shot, you should be really aware of moving your feet in such a way that you almost launch yourself into the shot.

(c) . . . out in front of the body.

(d) Keep the racquet face closed.

(e) Full follow-through.

(c) . . . out in front of the body.

(d) Keep the racquet face closed.

(e) Full follow-through.

Seek to play the ball well above net-height, taking it out in front. As you swing the racquet, close the face of the racquet on the ball.

You should be conscious of bending your knees, as the elevation created by the spring action will give you that little extra power. There should be no holding back on the follow-through either.

The Lob Volley

This is arguably one of the most difficult shots in the game. It is invariably used as a 'get out of jail' shot, and it requires such precision that if it is not executed properly, you are almost certain to find the opposition smashing the ball away for a winner.

The lob volley is used when players on both sides are in net positions. It is a shot that is generally played on impulse – generated by the closeness at the net of the players – and requires an excellent touch. The lob volley is probably used more in doubles than in singles. Use the shot sparingly and the surprise element can be rewarding.

You will be in a volley position, but because so little time is available, you will be playing the shot on reflex and so there will be little or no backswing. Play the ball well out in front of the body and brace the wrist on impact with an open racquet face. This will give you the necessary lift to create the lob.

Because of the angle of the racquet face, there will always be an element of backspin when playing this shot.

Due to the nature of the shot, there is also very little follow-through. When good players produce this shot, it can almost look as if they are flicking the ball off their racquet face.

The Low Volley
Figs 86 and 87

Arguably, as you improve your standard of tennis, the opposition will also be of a higher standard and will be able to impose their higher skills upon you. This will be especially apparent when you are at the net. Your opponent will be able to play topspin groundstrokes to make the ball dip lower over the net, which in turn means that the low volley will become an important part of your repertoire.

The most obvious difference between the high volley and the low volley is that, generally, the high volley is an

Fig 84   Zina Garrison playing a low forehand volley. She is leaning well forward, but retaining good balance.

Fig 85 Zina at full stretch, but still in control.

attacking shot. The low volley, on the other hand, because of the position from which it is being played, is a defensive shot. When playing the low volley – unless you are attempting the stop volley (*see* page 84) – you should endeavour to play the ball back into your opponent's court in such a way that it gets you back into the rally, hopefully in a position of control.

Do not try to be too ambitious with this shot, as it is not intended to be an outright winner. You are merely looking to play yourself back into a position of command.

In order to play the shot (*see* Figs 86 and 87) it is certainly necessary to have a short backswing, but the single most important point in playing a successful low volley is the ability to get down low to the ball. The need to bend the knees is absolutely imperative. Many of you will be surprised by how strong your thighs need to be to support the upper body for this shot.

Yet again, a very short blocking action is required to play the shot, with the ball being struck comfortably in front of the body. An open racquet face is a must because the ball is so low over the net.

Always play the shot with an element of backspin to give the control and feel necessary during its execution.

Fig 86 The low forehand volley.

(a)   Short backswing.

(b)   Bend the knees.

(c)   Get down to the ball.

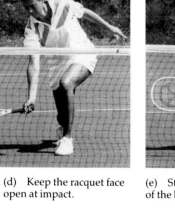

(d)   Keep the racquet face open at impact.

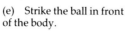

(e)   Strike the ball in front of the body.

(f)   Keep the knees bent throughout the shot.

Fig 87   The low backhand volley.

(a)   Short backswing.

(b)   Bend the knees to get down low to the ball.

(c)   Keep the racquet face open at impact.

(d)   Keep the knees bent throughout the shot.

Fig 88 Ivan Lendl – renowned for his powerful groundstrokes – improvises a deft dink.

The Dink

Very few books mention the dink, which is a shame, because when used successfully it can be very effective.

So what is the dink? It is almost a volley technique adapted to groundstroke play, and it can be used to great effect against a net player. If you have sufficient ability to combine the dink with an array of topspin ground-strokes, it can create all sorts of problems.

The subtle change between aggressive topspin and slow dinks, quite apart from causing the net player physical anguish, will also have a psychological effect on your opponent, making him feel insecure as to what is going to happen next.

The dink is used to absorb much of the pace of the ball coming to you. It therefore requires an excellent feel through the control of the racquet which gives you the ability to teasingly float the ball, very softly, low over the net.

It is very difficult to play against the dink, because you will probably already be at full stretch, playing a low volley with very little pace on the ball. You are therefore under pressure physically to get to the ball and then use your energy to create your own pace onto the ball. In all probability, an accomplished dinker will often follow up with the lob for his next shot.

The dink can cause all sorts of confusion and uncertainty, but be aware that if you do not play it competently, you will be setting up your opponent for an easy kill. It is a shot that requires a high degree of skill, coupled with the tactical awareness of knowing when to attempt it.

If you have any design on achieving success at doubles, the dink must be part of your repertoire of shots.

As suggested earlier, the dink is almost a volley technique adapted to groundstrokes. It will be difficult to play the dink with a Western forehand, so I suggest that if you want to learn to play this shot, you should choose the Eastern or Continental grip.

A very short backswing is required, so prepare to take the ball slightly out in front of the body with an open racquet face – which naturally creates the slice and sidespin necessary.

At impact, keep a firm but deft grip. This is the point at which the speed of the oncoming ball is absorbed, and you will need to combine your grip with the soft touch which is required to create the floating ball. Think of it as almost blocking the ball with a soft but positive follow-through.

The Under-Arm Serve

There are two occasions when an under-arm serve can be used:

1. When you have injured your shoulder and find it impossible to serve over-arm. If you are near the conclusion of the match it could in all probability be successful.
2. When it is used as a tactical ploy. There is a major misunderstanding about the use of the under-arm serve – you certainly do not have to inform the opposition of your intentions.

Quite simply, the under-arm serve is like doing an under-arm feed when knocking the ball back to your opponent. The two differences are that the ball must obviously go into the service box, and that you must strike the ball on the volley.

You can use forehand or backhand, and the most effective is the slice/sidespin serve which will keep the ball low on the court. If you use topspin it will sit up for your opponent to attack.

The Backhand Smash
Fig 89

This could well be the most difficult shot in the game. However, if you wish to be a successful net player, it really will be worth your while to add it to your repertoire.

The shot is used when you are not quick enough to reach the lob over your backhand side. If you want to retain the net position, you therefore have no other alternative but to use the backhand smash.

This shot requires superb agility, linked to strength in the wrist. You will not see a better exponent of the backhand smash than Yannick Noah.

The mechanics are as follows (see Fig 89). Quite obviously, a backhand grip will be required. Fast footwook is essential, and as you move you should create a very positive shoulder turn.

Seek out a very aggressive wrist action to attack, and bring the racquet face down on top of the ball. To obtain maximum effect, the ball should be in front of the body, as high as is possible without losing control.

Fig 89   The backhand smash.

(a)   Use the backhand grip.

(b)   Keep the feet moving and make a positive shoulder turn.

(c)   Seek out a very aggressive wrist action.

(d)   Fully extend the arm.

(e)   Reach up high.

(f)   Follow through.

The Round Arm Smash

One variation of the smash that is rarely used is the round arm smash. The greatest exponent of this is Jimmy Connors.

Use this shot when you are very reluctant to give up your attacking position at the net, but are not quick enough to play an orthodox smash. However, you can also use it when the lob is too high to play a conventional smash. The round arm smash is often used when you have been deceived or have misread a lob.

You will need very sharp footwork for this shot to get into a position where all your weight lies on the back foot.

Fig 90   Becker under extreme pressure, combining strength and athleticism whilst playing this awkward smash.

Because you will have little time to execute the shot, it is impossible to create a backscratch position. The arm will be completely extended in a bowling position for the shoulder to deliver the racquet head at the ball.

In all probability, when playing this shot you will be jumping off the ground in order to promote racquet-head speed at the ball. The whole action is similar to a cricketer's fast delivery.

9
SET-PIECES

We have covered all the strokes that make up a tennis player's armoury. Some players may be talented enough to be able to use all of the shots, while others will still be effective with a limited game.

Obviously it is up to you which range of shots you wish to use. In itself, being able to play good strokes does not necessarily mean that you will be a successful player. Selecting the right shot at the right time makes the difference between winners and losers. Being able to combine good technique with an astute tactical awareness is what makes fine match players.

The choice of shot is extremely personalized, but I do believe that it is worth discussing the important areas of the game, starting with the return of serve.

We have discussed the value of the serve and how several players have built their success around it (*see* Chapter 5). The same can also be said about the return of serve. Players of the calibre of Ken Rosewall, Jimmy Connors, Michael Chang, Jennifer Capriati, Chris Evert and Steffi Graf come to mind.

The ready position should be achieved between each shot, while awaiting serve or within a rally, just prior to executing the groundstroke or the volley, and this is an essential means of formulating your stroke. It enables you to prepare for your shot from a routine position.

Stand with your feet astride, just beyond shoulder-width apart. Lean forward from the

waist with your knees slightly bent and stand on the balls of your feet. Creating this stance is essential, as it will enable you to move swiftly and economically to the ball.

If you are at the baseline, you should stand approximately 60–90cm (2–3ft) behind it, and if at the net, you should be about 1.8–2.4m (6–8ft) from it. At all times be relaxed, and hold the racquet very lightly at the throat in your non-playing hand. I suggest that when you are at the net you should be supporting the racquet a little higher than you do at the baseline. The obvious reason for this is that the majority of volleys will be played about shoulder-height. If you are double-handed, you will probably start with your non-playing hand a little further down the grip.

When recovering from playing a wide shot, you will need to reposition yourself on the court, and the best way to do this is by remaining square-on to your opponent and using crab-like sideways movements. This retains good balance and allows you to be in a position from which you are able to move to any part of the court. It is worthwhile watching top class players doing this so effectively.

The Return of Serve

Statisticians draw attention time and time again to the missed return of serve on

crucial points. The return of serve is the first groundstroke that is played within a rally. However, in many circumstances it is probably the most difficult groundstroke you will make during the rally.

There are several reasons for this. The server is in control of where he will strike and place the serve. He is starting the rally off in his own time and is in command of the direction, pace and spin of the ball.

You, the returner, therefore have to be extremely alert. You must first be able to determine the direction, speed and flight of the ball and its probable bounce once it has struck the playing surface. Then, you have to make an immediate choice as to which method of groundstroke you wish to use.

The problem goes further, because you also have to gauge what the server will be doing next. Naturally, if the server stays on the baseline it will be wise to return the ball deep to his baseline to formulate a groundstroke rally. If the server chooses to come forward to launch a net attack, the reply to the serve would have to be adapted accordingly. You have the choice between an aggressive groundstroke down the line, a floater down the line, a groundstroke dipping at your opponent's feet or perhaps even a soft dink at his feet.

A word of advice for the server playing against a reputable returner of serve such as Chang or Seles. Do not panic and try to serve first-serve aces. You will probably not make enough of them to justify this method, however. You may surprise yourself if, instead, you reduce the quality of your first serve to make sure it goes in. This will prevent the returner receiving a high percentage of second serves to attack.

You may now be able to piece together the expertise required to be a successful returner of the serve. As a general rule, you will tend to adopt a more defensive attitude when playing against the first serve – for obvious reasons. However, as you grow in confidence, you may be able to reverse that situation against the second serve. Learn to take advantage of a weak second serve to launch your own attack; playing aggressive groundstrokes, hitting the weak serve aggressively into the corners, or playing an approach shot to take the net position.

The following guidelines will, I believe, provide food for thought and will help you develop your understanding of the return of serve.

Always give yourself a chance by seeking to return the ball into play. Many good players are guilty of unforced errors on the return of serve. If you are returning a weak serve, seek out your opponent's vulnerability by playing the ball into areas of the court he does not like, and this will put him on the defensive. At all times, try to keep the server guessing by varying the direction, pace and spin of your returns.

Naturally the style of groundstrokes you possess will affect your return of serve. If you have an extreme grip change, I suggest that you stand further back to give yourself more time to prepare for the shot, and then attempt to use your natural groundstrokes.

Always be aware of the wide-angled serve, because by standing further back you are creating the angle for it to be used against you. If the server sees that you have a large grip change he will probably seek to serve to a position which requires you to change the grip. Be aware of this tactical ploy.

At the same time, by standing further back you have created more time for yourself. Use that time wisely. Do not be frightened to use your aggressive groundstrokes, often with heavy topspin.

If you have a minimal grip change, you may be able to take the serve much earlier, often on the rise. You will have very little time to prepare, so use as little backswing as possible. Use the pace from the ball that is coming to you. Also, if you have a minimal grip change and are perceptive at picking up the flight and line of the oncoming serve, the combination of grip change and early sighting will enhance your threat to the server.

With this method, I cannot stress enough the need to get your body weight going forward to strike the ball out in front with a volley style action.

Tips

Certain practice routines or exercises will help to develop the return of serve. Do not take this stroke for granted. It is as important to work on returning serves as it is to spend hours drilling groundstrokes, or serves and volleys. If you really want to improve your tennis then you must find time to work on your returns. I am quite certain that you will be amazed at the benefits your game will gain from sensible and intelligent practice.

The key area is to understand the serve which is approaching you. How fast is it? What is its flight line? Is it flat, does it carry topspin or slice?

You will have to be perceptive and watch the ball very carefully as it comes off the server's racquet face. Being able to identify from an early stage the type of serve coming at you is therefore the first requirement in becoming an efficient returner of the ball.

Research the opposition. Get to know their favourite serve, and when they are likely to use it. Try to spot if they have any peculiar quirks which indicate where the ball will go. Look to where the server places the ball as this can very often indicate the style of serve he will use. The more alert and aware you become, the better.

Hopefully, these tips will help you develop a quick-thinking mind. Another essential requirement is good footwork. You should be ready to adjust to the wide swerving ball, the high-bouncing topspin serve and the ball that is delivered straight at your body.

Try to impose upon the server your own groundstroke strengths. Your opponent will naturally be aware of the shots you will favour, but by standing in certain positions you can intimidate and tempt him into serving to your strengths.

The mechanics will vary according to the type of shot you wish to play, and will also be linked to the grip and style you possess. However, the following requirements will apply to all styles.

Be at your most alert and be ready to move from a very

Fig 91   The tall Stefan Edberg gets down low for a backhand volley.

strong, balanced position. (Study good players and you will notice that they are leaning slightly forward on the balls of their feet when they are about to receive serve).

Be ready to move, with a diagonal movement, forward into the shot. At all times, try to strike the ball well in front of the body. It really does pay dividends to have your body weight going forward as you play the shot.

Always think in terms of making a quick recovery whilst playing the return of serve. According to the pace of the ball that is coming to you, vary the backswing. I suggest that the faster the serve, the shorter the backswing should be, and if you have more time, you may be able to use your full groundstroke.

When returning serve, be prepared to vary your tactics. No matter what style or method you play with, do not be afraid to experiment – taking the ball early, or standing well behind the baseline – because during your playing days, you will need to change your natural instincts at some time or other to counteract a particular style of server.

The Serve and Volley

If you like to base your game around a net attack, you will need to develop your serve and volley. Naturally, you will have to evolve a fine first serve, using weight of shot as well as a variety of spins to keep your opponent guessing. To have the confidence to serve and volley on your second serve, you will require a deep topspin serve of the highest calibre.

The Serve

The first area to examine if you want to be a successful serve and volleyer is the serve itself. Over the years I have seen players with very fine serves, but the stroke itself is not enough. The way in which they serve does not give them the elevation from the ground to carry them forward for a successful net attack.

One of the obvious modern day players who falls into this category is Ivan Lendl. He has an excellent serve, but he finds it difficult to use it as a means of moving forward towards the net.

Let me explain. If you watch natural serve and volleyers such as John McEnroe (*see* below), Boris Becker, Stefan Edberg, Pete Sampras or Martina Navratilova, you will observe that they are using the end of their service action to propel themselves forward. The movement that they

Fig 92   John McEnroe is an excellent example of a serve and volleyer who uses his momentum to carry him well into the net.

101

generate from their leg power during the serve projects them into the court at least 90 or 120cm (3 or 4ft). They are using that natural momentum to make their first move towards the net. Players who use that style of serve therefore combine a very effective service weapon with the forward momentum which is so necessary for an effective net attack.

If you are going to be a successful net player and use your serve as a means of attack to get to the net, you also need to consider the return of serve of your opponent. If your opponent plays an all-out, aggressive return, you will need to move much quicker to your net attack position in order to take away his opportunity to strike a winner cross-court, or down the lines. Use a little more spin and movement on your serve than you would normally, because if you hit a full-out flat serve and he has good timing, the ball will come back more quickly.

The second style of play you may come up against is the block, or dink, or floating return. This will give you two choices. If the ball is short and low, you will have to make very quick movements in order to set up an effective net attack. Alternatively, you can choose to wait and allow the ball to bounce and then play an approach shot.

You will notice that once a server has made his first move forward, he will usually achieve what is called a split position (i.e., with feet apart), just outside the service line. In effect, he is momentarily checking his stride and composing his balance and faculties. He will then make a very quick decision on whether he should move forward swiftly for the next shot or stay

back and play an approach shot.

It is the recognition of what to do at the right time which leads to a successsful net attack behind the serve. Obviously, the style of return from your opponent will help you make your decisions before you move forward. But there are several players on the professional tour who have a variety of shots, and so can keep their opponents guessing.

Another important factor in the serve and volley style is awareness of the angles created by the placement of your serve. For example, if you are serving from the right-hand court and serve wide towards the sideline, you cannot afford to give your opponent too much of a gap down the line as you approach the net. Therefore, you will move towards the net in such a way that you will give yourself the opportunity to cover the down-the-line passing shot.

By serving down the middle or a little towards your opponent's body, you will be creating less angle for him to use, and your approach to the net will be able to carry a central line of attack. At the same time, be aware of your opponent's preferred return.

If you are serving from the left-hand court and you serve wide, you will again have to cover the down-the-line passing shot, and the same ploy would occur if you were serving down the middle or at your opponent's body. You will approach the net very much more centrally and guard against the opposition's favourite return.

The Volley

If you are going to be a successful net player, you have to accept that by the very

virtue of going to the net, you are forcing your opponent to play a counter-attacking game. Therefore, your opponent will on occasions be successful himself by playing the winning groundstroke or the winning lob. It is of paramount importance to realize and accept that you are also going to be beaten on a percentage of the points.

You must, however, trust in your ability to go forward and force your opponent into errors or weak returns. You must never be frightened or discouraged if you are passed. The law of averages will allow for your opponent to be successful on occasions, and you must accept it.

It is worth bearing in mind that sometimes your opponent may feel that he does not have an opening and he might then blast the ball straight at your body, so having a quick mind and swift reflexes is important.

Another major aspect of attacking at the net is that there will be times when you have not selected the right shot or the right time to go forward, therefore putting yourself in a vulnerable position. However, try and work on what we call the bluff play. Guess which way your opponent is likely to strike the ball and move to that position just as he is about to hit it. You will be surprised how many times your guess proves right.

Study some fine net players the next time you have the opportunity, and you will see they can sometimes be beaten by 1.8 or 2.4m (6 or 8ft). They sometimes make mistakes, they guess the wrong way, but it does not stop them maintaining their attack.

So, to be a successful net player, always have the confidence to go forward. However, this is not an excuse for recklessness. There will be occasions when your serve is too short or slightly mis-hit, and if this happens, it is often wise to return to the baseline rather than rushing to the net.

By trial and error, you will begin to learn your angles better, or you will begin to learn the likely angles your opponent can create with his returns.

The Conversion Zone

Your game is developing, you have an understanding of all aspects of technique and in all probability you are beginning to make choices. You might be an out-and-out backcourt player, a serve and volleyer or an all-rounder, and I have hopefully given you some ideas about the return of serve.

There is now one particular factor I would like to discuss on which we have not touched yet. I have had the privilege of watching the majority of the greatest players of recent years and I am convinced that this is one critical area which gives them that little extra edge. Whatever style they use, all those players are deadly in the area which I call the 'conversion zone'. So, what is the conversion zone?

During the ebb and flow of a rally, there is generally a time when there is an opportunity to attack the ball and force the opposition onto the defensive. It is those players who, over a lengthy period of time, have the courage to take advantage of the situation, who become successful. There are times when the wrong decision is taken, but taking a risk is where courage comes into play.

There is no obvious area which can be called the conversion zone, but in all probability, any ball that lands within 60–90cm (2–3ft) of either side of the service line will be deemed to be within it (*see* Fig 94).

There are three ways of approaching the ball in this area. You can:

1. Play the ball safely back into court and let the rally continue.
2. Go for a groundstroke winner, which might be struck aggressively ninety per cent of the time, and might be a drop shot ten per cent of the time (*see* Fig 95).
3. Play an approach shot to gain a net position.·

The higher the standard of tennis you are playing, the fewer opportunities you will find to put your opponent under pressure. It therefore

Fig 93   Notice how Becker is about to lean into his studied backhand approach.

103

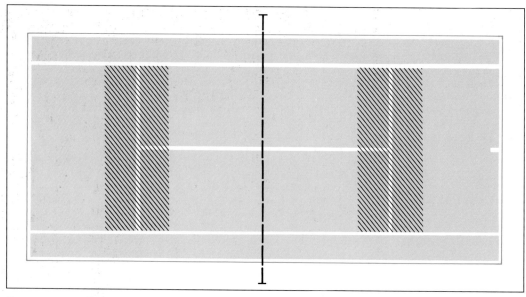

Fig 94   The 'conversion zone'.

follows that the more confident you are of playing the ball in the conversion zone, the greater your chance of winning will be.

The Groundstroke Winner

It really is worth watching players such as Jennifer Capriati and Ivan Lendl, who are regarded as efficient backcourt machines. Having battled hard during a 30-stroke rally to find the ball in the conversion zone, they will not fight shy of attacking it, probably going for a winner deep to one of the baseline corners. It is their trademark. They display an incredible patience linked to a very sound knowledge of when to attack.

Many people ask themselves how Bjorn Borg could ever win on grass with many highly competitive serve and volley exponents lined up against him. The amount of volleys he played during the championships were negligible, but whenever the ball was in the conversion zone, he would hit very

aggressive topspin groundstroke winners.

To play aggressively in this area, a slight adaptation to your technique is needed. Obviously, you are playing the ball closer to the net than you would with a normal groundstroke, so an early backswing is vital and it is imperative to position yourself so that you are able to put your weight behind the shot. Unless the ball is particularly high – when a full groundstroke can be played – the adaptation occurs by having a shorter backswing.

The shot you play is really up to you. It can be a firm slice or a whippy topspin. Whatever it is, the key factor is your attitude. Be brave. Be positive.

There will be times when you make the wrong decision. That is inevitable, so do not let it dwell on your mind. If a ball arrives similar to one you have just missed, learn to have a positive attitude. Grab the bull by the horns and go for it again. It will pay dividends in the long term.

The Approach Shot

The other method of playing the ball in the conversion zone is the approach shot, to place your opponent under pressure with a net attack. I have seen many players, however, fall foul of attempting too difficult a shot. Remember, if you are looking to win the point from the net, you should be an adequate volleyer. Trust in your ability to volley successfully after playing the approach shot. If the approach shot in itself is a winner, that is a bonus.

Trust in your volleying to complement your approach play. Players who use this method successfully – and are well worth watching to improve your understanding of this tactic – are John McEnroe, Stefan Edberg and Martina Navratilova. Also, look out for somebody like Pam Shriver, who with relatively poor groundstrokes has nevertheless succeeded because of a very astute understanding of how to go to the net.

Fig 95 Martina Navratilova shows remarkable flexibility in playing an awkward ball in the conversion zone.

Fig 96   Steffi Graf preparing to play a sliced backhand. Note the racquet head above the wrist.

One important attribute that good net players possess is the ability not to get disturbed whenever they are passed. They will obviously not select the correct ball on every sortie to the net, but their confidence in pressing for the net position to beat the opposition will not be dented.

Be aware, when approaching the net, that a large percentage of the time you will be playing the ball while you are moving forward, so it is essential to be well balanced while playing the shot.

Keep mentally very alert, on the look-out for the tell-tale signs that the ball is going to be short enough to be attacked.

I would suggest that the most effective way to play an approach shot is by using slice and sidespin, because the combination of both spins keeps the ball low and moving away from your opponent. This will mean that the groundstroker will have to hit from below the level of the net when attempting his passing shots.

When using the slice approach shot, you really need to get up to the ball, almost as if you are on top of it as you play it. Early preparation of the racquet is vital, and when using slice, open the racquet face to produce the necessary spin required. The shorter the backswing, the better, and be firm with the forward swing of the racquet.

There will be occasions when you could use topspin, but choose them very carefully.

The conversion zone is rather an abstract area. It really is the individual player's own way of seeking out attack, depending on his own attitude to risk. Experiment. Try to discover what the right method is for you. Be prepared for disap-pointment, but keep trying.

10
INDIVIDUALITY

One of the exciting areas in tennis is how individuals interpret the mechanics of the game in different ways. We have discussed very thoroughly the basic techniques necessary to play tennis, but what makes it an interesting game is the individual's own interpretation of how his strokes should be formed.

Naturally, the way you grip the racquet and the style of play you use – and by that I mean whether you are a backcourt or a net player – will determine the shapes that you create to strike a tennis ball.

As a tennis teacher, this area particularly concerns me. Many coaches have a firm belief in teaching very rigid methods and pay no regard to the individualistic leanings of their pupil. I am not suggesting that changes of style to their pupil's game will not be beneficial, but what I am suggesting is that they should look at the best way to teach each individual person.

There are two common factors within a reliable technique:

1. The ability, time and time again, to produce a shape of stroke which will not break down when placed under repeated pressure.
2. The ability to control the racquet face consistently at impact with the ball.

When learning the mechanics of a particular stroke, be aware that you are creating a shape for your own stroke production. Seek the ability to practise diligently and wisely at all times, trying to learn a shape of stroke that will work effectively for you.

As mentioned earlier when discussing the top players' methods, there are several shapes that can be formed when preparing your strokes. Learn which is the right one for you. Experiment. Is it a straight takeback, is it a shallow loop, is it a large loop? You can only find out through practice.

Disguise

Discussing shape and stroke formation brings me into another area, and this is disguise. It is the ability to

---

Stroke Formation

If we take a cross-section of the top players of recent times and look at their strokes, we will notice the wide variety of stroke formations that are used.

Four top women players are Chris Evert, Steffi Graf, Gabriela Sabatini and Martina Navratilova.

Evert's stroke production is very simple. She takes her racquet back on both her groundstroke wings with the straight takeback method, which very much reflects a 'taught' style.

Graf's forehand preparation is with a flurry across her body. She then creates a high takeback which enables her to get the loop into her aggressive topspin forehand.

Sabatini's forehand is a very wristy action, and her trademark is the follow-through, in which she finishes with the racquet over her playing shoulder (see Fig 57). Her body weight almost goes against the swinging action of her arm.

Navratilova's forehand is a fairly simple stroke which relies on a small loop to induce the forward swing.

Now let us look at four of the men. Ivan Lendl, Jimmy Connors, John McEnroe and Boris Becker.

Lendl tends to be the exception to the rule these days and favours a firm base from which to hit his powerful groundstrokes. His stroke production is fairly simple, with a shallow loop which allows him to play with a very strong forearm/wrist action.

Connors tends to be unique on his forehand side in that he almost prepares with a slight underswing on the takeback, which is one of the reasons why he plays with very little margin of error on his forehand side.

In McEnroe, we have a genius who plays with beautiful hand control over the racquet and a unique short, lazy takeback which appears almost nonchalant and careless as he prepares for the shot. This, however, suits his very individualistic skills.

Becker prepares with a very sharp, looped takeback to create the room he needs to play his aggressive topspin groundstrokes.

I have given you a cross-section of eight of the most powerful players in the game and, as you can see, they have each developed their own way to strike a tennis ball.

Fig 97   Capriati's early preparation gives her the opportunity to play a backhand drive or topspin lob. This is the value of disguise.

conceal from your opponent the type of shot you are about to play – something the best players have got down to a fine art.

Learning the value of how to shape your strokes consistently around your own individual style will help you to develop one of the fundamental skills that promotes disguise.

This leads us into the value of good hand control of the racquet. Disguise your shot by shaping the stroke in such a way that your opponent cannot see what you are going to do with the ball until the very last moment. That, coupled with the delay of the hand use of the racquet, will give you the facility to keep your opponent guessing.

Hand Skills

You may ask what hand skill is. It is the ability, within the framework of a stroke, to add subtle changes to the intended direction of the ball by closing or opening and thus altering the angle of the racquet face with last-moment hand adjustments.

Can this be taught? Earlier, I was very careful about discussing in depth how tightly you should hold the racquet at impact. It is quite obvious that to be in control of the racquet at impact, it is necessary to have a secure grip to provide constant ball strike.

However, I fervently believe that the lighter the racquet is held prior to the strike, the better, as it allows greater freedom to use the wrist in producing delicate manipulations of the racquet head. A light hold of the racquet is absolutely essential if you are going to be able to cater for this last-moment delay, and it is vital in developing your hand skills.

Fig 98   Ivan Lendl, showing great hand skill and quick reactions.

Due to the lighter materials now available and the construction processes of the modern racquet, it is easier to gain good hand skills. Only some twenty-five years ago, the theory used to be as big a grip and as heavy a racquet as possible. These two factors forced a player to grip the racquet very tightly. This created styles which produced power, but prevented the easy manoeuvrability which is commonly available with the racquets used today.

Let me give you two good examples of the way in which a light hold gives a good effect. When writing with a pencil and if gripping too tightly, you would not be able to write fluently. Secondly, you would not be effective if you gripped a dart too tightly before launching it at its target.

As the game is developing and the standards are improving, one requirement that has come to the fore is the

109

necessity to become faster in many facets of the game. Much quicker reflexes are needed and the equipment available today responds to that need (*see* Fig 98). As far as hand skills are concerned, this means being able to manipulate the racquet much more quickly.

There are no hard and fast rules about developing hand skills – have fun and experiment. When playing, observe how early you wish to grip the racquet when playing your stroke. Try to leave it as late as possible before applying your grip pressure to the handle of the racquet. Sometimes, do not even grip the racquet at all. Just hold it lightly throughout the stroke and find out the effect the ball has on the racquet face at impact.

Under the pressures of match play, if you grip the racquet tightly, too early, it will set up tension in your arm. This will be counter-productive

to producing a smooth swing of the racquet at the vital moment, and can lead to injury.

Taking The Ball Early

When you feel at ease and in control of striking the ball regularly at waist-height, it will be extremely beneficial to learn to strike the ball earlier. Without doubt, this is a common feature in the game of the top players, and with many more tournaments being played on a cement-based surface, which promotes a high-bouncing ball, I would argue that any player who wishes to pursue a professional career must have the ability to take the ball early.

The advantages of striking the ball earlier than normal are that you are giving your opponent less time to prepare for his next shot. If you are capable of doing this consistently, you will probably cause your opponent to panic under the pressure and he will consequently hit a poor shot. Another advantage is that you will now be controlling the rallies and will therefore be less vulnerable to attack. A prime exponent of this method of play is Steffi Graf, who can often be seen consistently hitting very aggressive early ball winners from 90–120cm (3–4ft) inside her baseline.

This brings me to another fine player who has emerged from the US, Jennifer Capriati (*see* Fig 97), who already had the capacity at thirteen years of age to strike an excellent early ball from both her forehand and her double-handed backhand with devastating effect.

Due to the style of play in the men's game, it would be almost impossible to survive

Fig 99 Edberg, famous for his backhand, executes a very difficult early ball.

110

Fig 100   The 'off-forehand' shot.

without the ability to take the ball early.

A striking feature that is emerging from the early ball prowess is the 'off shot'. To date, the off shot has predominantly been hit off the forehand, although one of Jennifer Capriati's strengths is her ability to play these shots from her backhand wing as well. For simplicity's sake, I will concentrate on the 'off forehand'.

This is played when there is sufficient time to get into position to play a forehand when the ball is travelling to your backhand wing. In all probability, your stance will be open and you will be striking the ball early, aggressively and at an angle, as shown in Fig 100.

The other obvious feature apart from the shot being aggressive is that it will usually take your opponent completely by surprise. Also, by preparing yourself for this shot, you will

still have the option to play the ball cross-court. However, be aware that this is a high-risk shot and so requires:

a)   Confidence
b)   Plenty of practice

Whilst on the subject of taking the ball early, especially on cement courts, it is important to realize the disadvantage of allowing the ball to fall from the top of its bounce to approximately waist-height, as you will find yourself a couple

111

Fig 101   In order to develop her career, Sabatini has worked hard to improve her volley.

of metres behind the baseline in a defensive position.

To play an early ball, you will probably have to adapt your technique. It will certainly not be easy to have a large loop and be effective playing these shots.

The shorter and simpler the takeback, the easier it will be to adapt to taking the ball early.

112

11
MOBILITY

Hopefully, you now have a picture of the basic technical skills needed to play the game of tennis, complemented by an understanding of shape of stroke and a knowledge of how to obtain the best out of your own particular style.

This leads me on to one area which I personally feel is the most important facet of playing the game well; and that is mobility.

Right from the word go, it must be stressed to anyone wanting to play that tennis is a very mobile game.

Once you feel comfortable with the game and are learning the basic methods of hitting the ball, the need for footwork becomes all too apparent and should be quickly emphasized.

Footwork involves moving to and around the ball, hence the need early in the teaching process to use your feet effectively. All too often, players become mechanically, and solely, oriented to the swing and the grip.

Let Technique
Take a Back-Seat

Generally speaking, many coaches who work at the early stage in the development of players are guilty of becoming obsessed with technical development, while neglecting the immense value of footwork.

I have seen so many frustrated tennis players who cannot combine methods and techniques with their

Fig 102 Michael Chang, whose feet say more than words!

footwork, because their early teaching has been geared towards mechanics with too little attention being paid to footwork.

I personally would rather work with a player who moves very ably, but with poor mechanics, than with a player with good mechanics and poor

113

footwork. In my experience, it is far easier to mould technique into able footwork than vice versa.

The other interesting factor here is boredom. Pupils have much more fun merging their mechanics into able footwork than performing in almost robot-like fashion, merely learning technique around perfect ball-feeding.

When I look at beginners trying to play, I find that one of the most difficult things for them to relate to is the regimentation of technique and the co-ordination of movement. They are forming their strokes in a wooden manner, with a poor appreciation of the moving ball.

The Front Foot

This leads me to one of the most important areas of technical teaching: what I call the pre-setting of the front foot. I am certain that a premature setting of the front foot will encourage poor footwork, poor co-ordination and lead to eventual frustration.

When teaching technique, the key from the outset is to make the player feel happy about his movement and help him get the racquet to the ball on a regular basis. He should be encouraged to get the greatest effectiveness out of his shot-making by transferring his weight forward into the ball.

If you study the top players, you will notice – apart from when they play the sliced backhand – how well they can hit the ball off the back foot, or with both feet off the ground. Yet, they are still able to project their weight forward (*see* Fig 103).

This is one of the keys to

Fig 103 Although Jo has been caught playing the shot off the back foot, she retains excellent balance and poise, and still projects her upper body weight forward.

playing well: always project your weight into the shot. Now, it does not necessarily follow that if you set the front foot before the ball arrives that your weight will automatically transfer forward.

The major danger, and I might add common failing, of pre-setting the front foot is that if you misjudge the movement and flight of the ball, even by a

minimal amount, you will not have time to readjust the position of your feet. Consequently, your body reacts to your swing by falling away from the shot.

It is imperative to understand that the art of successful and effective weight transference is to move in such a way that your weight lies on the back foot until it transfers

Fig 104   The photograph speaks for itself!

forward, in conjunction with the forward swing of the racquet. In that way, you will obtain effective use of the front foot as it plays a role in the stroke.

However, as mentioned earlier, many of today's great players will play their groundstrokes off the back foot or with both feet off the ground. It is impossible, since the game is being played at such speed and momentum, to always produce what I would call text book technique.

If you tried to manipulate your footwork to play every shot on the front foot, you would simply find yourself running out of time for each shot. Be aware, when watching international tennis players, of the way in which their shot-making and recovery for the next shot merge into one movement.

Study how a player such as Steffi Graf hits as many as eighty per cent of her forehands in elevation.

This particular style of play is not just beneficial to the better players. Your tennis will flow much better if you are less paranoid about setting the front foot too soon before the ball arrives.

In my opinion, the front foot setting routine is totally counter-productive to creating fluency and mobility.

Co-Ordinating Movement

Good players seem able to co-ordinate the production of both movement and stroke and to make it look easy. While they are producing their stroke, they have no problem moving their feet. Like patting your head and rubbing your stomach at the same time, all you need is practice.

Many people can produce strokes, but find it uncomfortable to move their feet. So, if you really want to develop your tennis in a successful manner, make learning to move an enjoyable but demanding priority, and this as early as possible.

There is some confusion about movement. You can break tennis movements down into three categories:

1.   Chasing the ball. This, quite frankly, should occur instinctively if you wish to play tennis to any level.

2.   Moving around the ball. This, in my experience, is a problem area.

3.   Agility. This is closely related to moving around the ball, and includes jumping, leaping, diving and recovery.

An area of paramount importance is being able to create room to hit your shots. We discussed previously the need to assess the flight of a ball if you are hitting a groundstroke. Let the ball bounce, rise and fall, and strike it at waist-height. Focus on that particular area: your eyes are telling you about the flight of the ball.

In consequence, you have an understanding of where the ball should be positioned to strike it effectively. Almost automatically, in conjunction with watching the ball in flight, information is passed to the brain, which instinctively sets the feet moving. You must understand that if you do not move in co-ordination with what your eyes are telling you, you are going to find the game terribly difficult.

You cannot even begin to achieve any success in the game at any level, unless your feet want to move. This brings us to anticipation and vision, and these two points can definitely be learnt.

Anticipation and Vision

Your eyes are an essential tool in learning how to move, because they will be telling you what the ball is doing. They will be informing you of flight, spin and speed of the ball, as well as the length and width of the court and where the ball is going to land.

You must also be aware of

Fig 105   Martina Navratilova. Note the use of the non-playing hand for balance.

Fig 106   Zina Garrison – a beautiful mover.

Fig 107   Michael Chang at full stretch, sliding on a clay court to play an extremely difficult low forehand.

Fig 108   Nobody anticipates better than McEnroe at his best.

angles and shapes of strokes are produced. It will help you to anticipate better (*see* Fig 108).

Too many people only start to worry about the ball when it comes over their side of the net, but you should already be aware of what it is doing as it leaves the opponent's racquet.

Part of anticipation comes from hearing the sound of the ball off the racquet. We take for granted hearing the sound of the ball. Experiment by putting some cotton wool in your ears and you will be astonished how your reaction time will change. Many players taking part in the US Open complain of this noise problem – caused by the scream of jets taking off over the courts from a nearby airport.

Athletic Training

It may be that with more money available and with the public's higher expectations of top level tennis, players have a greater desire to perform at their best and are seeking out any means by which to achieve better performances.

The coach travels full-time with perhaps seventy-five per cent of the top players. Many players also seek out fitness trainers, in the shape of athletic trainers.

Athletic trainers are able to develop a player's muscles and improve his stamina. Ironically, however, I have yet to identify many tennis players who have gained any noticeable increase in speed from athletic training.

This is perhaps explained by the fact that athletic disciplines require strong powerful movements which rely on pumping arms and legs, always running in straight lines. Reflexes and anticipation play little role apart from the athlete's reactions to a starting pistol.

what your opponent is doing with his racquet. The shape of strokes he uses, linked to racquet face angles will determine how the ball will react at your end.

Therefore, learning to understand how your opponent produces and puts his shots into effect will give you an early start in being able to react and move to where the ball will land on your side of the court.

So now we know that many

players who are described as fast movers on the court are not just moving their feet well, but are responding to an early recognition of what their opponent is doing as they hit the ball. They see very early what is going on.

It is well worth going to matches and focusing on one particular player. Before he strikes the ball, try and work out where the ball is going to land in the opposition's half. You will start to learn what

Movement

Lennie Heppell is a former professional rock 'n roll champion of Great Britain. Once a coal miner, he opened a night club, and through his love of dancing he became fascinated in good movement.

His daughter Maureen became an international table tennis player and in working with her he recognized his talent for improving movement within sport. His knowledge has made him much in demand in the international world of sport, and he has worked in particular with many of England's top footballers and hockey players, as well as with tennis players. This is his advice:

Good tennis movement is about being comfortable at all times with your own body in relation to the ball. To achieve that, you have to develop animated movement from your head and neck right down to your feet. A poor player will think that as long as he gets his footwork right, then everything will be OK, but the game is about knowing how to *move* as opposed to knowing how to run.

Running comes naturally when you are a child, but as you get older the upper body becomes stiffer. Throughout your life you are taught bad habits, or rather habits that inhibit fluid movement, habits that prevent you being light on your feet. You really have to reject what you might have been told all your life by parents or teachers about standing up straight and pulling your shoulders back.

Stiffness is out. When you watch people walk, you will notice a tension in the back, but to be comfortable with your own body in relation to a ball, it is important to be physically relaxed.

There is not enough movement in the shoulders. You have to learn to walk with a pendulum action. To understand this, imagine you are walking astride a plank about 15cm (6in) wide. It will help the body roll a little better.

You have to learn how to run backwards, how to move sideways and how to move forward. Being a good track athlete has nothing at all to do with being a good, athletic tennis player. Athletes learn to run in a straight line with no flexibility of movement from side to side. In tennis, you have to link your training to the movement of a ball and not just to power and strength.

Many coaches are very guilty of teaching players mechanics and technique without linking the two to movement. Players are taught how to hit the ball, but not how to move to meet the ball. Movement must come first. Practise this with the coach feeding balls in various positions on the court and encouraging you to run. When, and only when, fluency occurs should technique be taught around movement.

Now visualize a tennis player. Because of the dimensions of a tennis court he is looking to cover short distances, running with a low centre of gravity, with a racquet in hand, to produce a stroke to strike the ball. Because he is having to form a stroke around the ball when he meets it, his footwork pattern will be broken up into short steps. All this is occurring within 4 or 6m (15 or 20ft), so quick reflex, response and recovery are the key factors in a good tennis player's movements.

I have had the good fortune to work with a movement expert, Lennie Heppell, who has come up with some superb observations (*see* above and on the next three pages). In my experience, many athletic trainers simply do not understand the types of movement that are required for tennis. I believe they should be able to divorce themselves from the style of training that sprinters, hurdlers, long jumpers and so on would use, because each sport – not just tennis – has its own specialized movements.

As already stated, many athletic trainers are obsessed with legs pumping, arms pumping and bringing the knees up high in training routines, and these are totally destructive movements for tennis.

So, be very selective if you decide to use an athletic trainer.

This is not to say that tennis players are not athletic. A tennis player is a good athlete within his own sport. By the same token, although he is a good tennis athlete, he is not necessarily proficient at athletic disciplines.

Liquid Rhythm

It is no use just getting the arms pumping and the knees up. You have to be able to learn how to go after the ball with quick, reflex movements, and the best way to learn that is not with a straight back.

Upper-body strength is good for a stronger grip and stronger arm for the power part of hitting the ball, but it does not help movement. You need what I call 'liquid rhythm'. Your body has to be very supple to get a feel of spreading in the movement. You have to be slinky.

Sticking your backside out is of great benefit both to tennis players and footballers. It gives a better body shape, which in turn improves stroke production, and is also very important in assisting you to turn and move when necessary. If you watch toddlers when they have just started walking, they will do this naturally. It acts like a rudder and gives you balance and support in the upper body. Zina Garrison is an excellent example, and she is one of the fastest movers you can find on a tennis court.

Side movement can be helped by a kind of Egyptian dance method. Keep the head level and the shoulders completely relaxed, and then move the head from side to side. This gives good balance in sideways movement.

Go into any movement with an open stance, because it allows you the facility of making any final adjustments.

If you are serious about trying to improve your tennis, whatever your level, you should look at the way you walk or hold yourself away from the tennis court.

If you are carrying an awkward stance and your movement is awkward, then it is damaging your capabilities in the game.

Learning how to walk properly is more difficult than doing an exercise on the tennis court. You can practise the correct posture all the time – as you go to school or fetch the shopping, for instance. You have to learn to glide. Some players, like Michael Chang and Miloslav Mecir have made it look easy.

These theories are not in opposition to the tried-and-tested training methods, but rather add to them – an alternative medicine, if you like.

Fig 109   Pat Cash's trademark – a diving volley.

Fig 110   Steffi Graf, the most mobile player in the women's game, can be seen here
confirming Lennie Heppell's observations.

Alertness and Rhythm

We are only born with so much natural rhythm and harmony, and we have to continually search for and develop ways of maintaining both if our performance and movement are to be consistent. This body machine of ours, like any other mechanical machine or instrument, needs constant servicing and tuning if it is to be kept together in rhythm and harmony. Total co-ordination in movement should resemble a fish in water – a flip of its tail and off it goes, changing pace and direction with ease.

My fifty years' experience in teaching and encouraging top sports people how to alert and organize muscular harmony and fluency of movement has enabled me to obtain dramatic and successful results. These movements of alertness and rhythm I term 'miniature body rhythm'. Because of the small amount of motion involved, these movements are hardly noticeable, but they are there!

Never start moving from an inert position, because movements that are jerky and lack rhythm and fluency create a start-and-run action instead of a sway-and-drift action. All the great movers who come to mind – Pele, Mohammed Ali, Sam Snead, Bjorn Borg, Fred Astaire and so on – started with movements that were smooth, sweet, fluid and perfectly balanced. They flowed. Many young players might be able to get by for a few years without a preliminary awareness of 'miniature body rhythm', but developing it is an absolute must if they want to reach the higher realms of their profession.

In order to move to a ball, you have to be physically, as well as mentally, ready to move. The rhythm, timing and harmony between mind and body starts well before you reach the ball.

You must alert the body and make it aware, as you would your fingers that were about to pick something up. Your body, like your fingers, must be sensitive to touch. Many bad movements and missed shots are caused by nerves, tension and tightness, and these can be minimized by developing a lifestyle around 'miniature body rhythm'. I do not want to be discouraging, but learning to develop this skill is not easy. It takes special dedication. If you are too tense, you will often appear a little awkward at first, but with practice and better style movement, you will develop your own tempo in movement. Eventually, the result will show up in a better and more consistent performance.

The sequence featured here clearly demonstrates the upper-body flight (or movement) which is so vital to the development of quick sideways movement. It is needed in all aspects of tennis mobility, but none more so than in the first move, when having to cover a lot of ground in order to reach wide balls, and when moving quickly to the wide volleys.

It is a big misconception to move the feet first. There is approximately a 15cm (6in) movement of the body before the feet move as a response to the upper-body movement. Stand still, and then make a move in any direction. Try moving the feet first, and then try it with the top part of your body, and you will see which is easiest. The body should always lead the feet, and not the other way around. The upper body (including the head) forms the heaviest part of you, and so you have to initiate the movement there, otherwise, that part of the body gets left behind.

The upper-body flight can be developed through some simple exercises. First of all, start with your feet shoulder-width apart. Now, without moving your feet at all, slide your head, neck and shoulders to the right. Hold the position for a count of five, and then repeat this movement to the left. Try to keep your shoulders level at all times and also keep your head upright. You should feel the stretch right through your neck and shoulder muscles.

As you become accustomed to doing this exercise you will be able to slide your head and shoulders from side to side with a sharper movement. It will also train your body to be in the correct balanced position for tennis. As you can see from Fig 111, it helps to practise with your arms held out to the sides, as this keeps your shoulders level and gives you more control over your balance. If you can practise this simple movement for a few minutes each day it will help you progress to the third movement. All this involves is a single step to one side, following the movement of your upper body. Practise this small step to both forehand and backhand sides, but remember: your head, neck and shoulders move first!

Now you are ready to go to the court and show off your new speed, balance and control to your fellow players. But do not forget to keep practising, on and off the court.

Fig 111

Figs 111–114   Lennie Heppell.

Fig 112

Fig 113

Fig 114

Fig 115   Boris Becker diving full length for a wide volley.

Fig 116   Perfect demonstration of a combination of strength and agility, as James Lenton leaps for a wide backhand volley.

Agility

Agility is something that has to be looked at more in tennis. If you are going to be a fine net player, you need to be able to make the recovery and then make the movement, for example, of moving from a low forehand volley to a high

backhand volley or to a smash. You need good reactions and good agility. Prime examples would be Boris Becker, Pat Cash and Martina Navratilova.

There is simply not enough understanding of agility within the game. You can cover 1.80–2.70m (2–3yd) with one

powerful, agile move (*see* above). Goalkeepers would make good net players. Visualize Peter Shilton, the former England goalkeeper making a reflex save and at the same time visualize Stefan Edberg picking off a wide volley.

125

12
MORE ON TECHNIQUE

We have examined all of the pertinent areas relating to a basic understanding of the game. We have discussed mechanics, grips, swings and footwork. However, certain areas need to be re-emphasized.

What is good technique? What do good players do well? What do they all have in common?

1.   Good vision and anticipation.
2.   Speed of movement in all directions, with the ability to change direction, plus good footwork around the ball linked to good body movement. (People always seem to misconstrue footwork as ball chasing, but it means having the ability to move around the ball well to create the room necessary to produce the shot.)
3.   Early preparation of the racquet, whilst moving.
4.   Disguise of shot.

All these areas require time and good players always seem to have time. There is no doubt that if the first three points mentioned above are working for you, you can have the time available to disguise your shot. Producing regular, consistent shapes gives you time and the conditions to be able to disguise what is going to happen next. The shapes will vary from player to player, but each particular style will have its own uniform shape, which will be produced time and time again, so that the opposition

cannot see if the ball is going down the line or cross-court.

A Little More . . .

1.   Top players have the ability to survive physically. They work hard on their practice routines and drilling, in such a manner that their matches appear easy.
2.   Away from the court, a large majority of today's top players also pursue other areas which lead to improving their physical condition, such as weight training, running, cycling and even aerobics. The pressure of having to play a tough three- or five-set match means that those who are stronger physically are probably mentally stronger too. The odds are that they are not having to tax themselves mentally, if they feel they can cope physically.
3.   Concentration and consistency. These two factors go hand in hand.
4.   Accuracy. Players of a high calibre are capable of repeatedly hitting the ball to a constant and accurate length, and appear to have the ability under pressure to thread the ball through the eye of a needle.
5.   The ability to take an early ball consistently.
6.   Confidence. You almost get the impression that top class players look forward to crisis situations in matches. It is a time when they must be courageous and believe in their ability to win over the situation.

The earlier you can develop

the confidence to play the crisis points (the big points) well, the more will you be able to cope with pressure throughout your playing days. Good players simply do not appear to be frightened of making mistakes on the big points.

Whichever style you choose to play with, you must have the courage to believe in yourself at all times.

We are obviously discussing an individual's strength of character and I cannot stress enough the importance of working on, and developing your mental attitude. This is such a large and important area that a separate section is devoted to the mental approach (*see* Part 5).
7.   Recovery. By this, I do not just mean physical, but mental and tactical as well. It really is worth watching two evenly matched opponents in combat. You will observe how, during the course of a long rally, both parties are capable of reversing defence into attack.

One player can be under extreme pressure, with seemingly little chance of surviving, and still less of winning the rally, but because of strong fighting instincts linked to excellent physical conditioning he will not only be able to get back into the rally, but also turn it to his advantage. There never appears to be a lost cause. Some matches seem poised for an inevitable victory for one party, and yet can be reversed, with the other party claiming victory two hours later.

13
UNDERSTANDING YOURSELF

You should now be developing game plans for your matches.

Be aware of your opponent's weaknesses and patiently and sensibly try to expose them. At the early stages, do not be over-ambitious. The overwhelming need is to keep the ball in court, while not leaving yourself open to attack – so, do not overpress.

Success does not depend entirely upon the quality of the strike. Occasionally, you will have the opportunity to delay your chosen shot, and by doing so you may wrong-foot your opponent. Alternatively, he may move into the position where he expects you will hit the ball, and your delaying the shot will allow you instead to play the ball to his original position. This is termed as playing the ball behind him.

Try and keep your opponent on the move. By applying this type of pressure, you will cause stress in his shot-making and ultimately, as he tires of chasing the ball, his judgement and quality of strike will deteriorate.

While playing matches, be aware of the quality of shot required to pressurize your opponent. It may be fun being aggressive and looking for winners, but on some occasions, there is no merit in it.

The sensible shot, played consistently, will cause damage to your opponent's game. This is called playing percentage tennis, and at whatever level you play, it is extremely important to understand the quality of shot which is likely to be successful. Even the most aggressive ball strikers are sensible and selective in the application of their shots.

Natural vs Method Play

Let us now turn to the pros and cons of being a 'natural' or a 'method' player.

The instinctive, natural player often finds it difficult to achieve his maximum capabilities. One of the problems he experiences is that, although he finds the game easy, he finds it mentally and physically difficult to train and work as hard as he should.

By contrast, the method player – the player with good timing, good technique, but limited flair and a lack of instinctive hand skills – has to work so hard to achieve success that he is prepared to sweat and work harder to reach his goal.

That is one point. Another difference becomes apparent in match play. The natural player finds himself at an advantage when under pressure – he will play instinctively on impulse and does not have to think too much about what is happening.

The method player, in this situation, finds himself restricted to one way of playing and can sometimes be lost for that little bit of flair, the surprise factor. He finds it more difficult to conjure up something to pull himself out of trouble.

The main danger that the natural player faces is when he has too much time to think. He has too many alternatives. One of the best tactics to use when you are playing someone who finds the game very easy, is to slow it down, to give him the choice and time to think and perhaps confuse himself. He is often looking for the most difficult shot – it is often part of his personality and he cannot resist playing the difficult shot.

The merit of the method player, is the fact that he has had to work so hard to achieve on his technique that his basics are sound. He may have a limited repertoire of shots, but he is able to use them consistently at all times. This means that when there is an opportunity for choice, he will stick to that rigid pattern of play. It makes the shots deliberate, but at the same time, he is probably less likely to miss them at times of high pressure.

It is my personal impression that the more natural and instinctive player also tends to be more vulnerable mentally. This is probably a reflection of his uncertainty over the choice of shot, as well as not spending the hours of dedication and application on his game.

The natural player tends to get more concerned with bad line calls. Ilie Nastase and Hana Mandlikova were both prime examples of the more gifted type of players – in terms of hand skills and

127

reactions – who seemed less able to cope mentally when the pressure increased.

On the other side of the coin, we have John McEnroe, who despite his outbursts over the years has proved that he could cope exceedingly well under pressure. However, it could be argued that he might have added more titles to his name by using a more disciplined approach.

Be Yourself

There is another aspect of the game which should be addressed. As mentioned earlier, there are any number of styles of play that might be used, and quite naturally there is a desire – especially among the very young – to try and copy their favourite player. But I believe in individuality. I am not suggesting that you should not pick up certain ideas which you can adapt to your own game. However, I have not yet seen anyone become successful by modelling their entire game on someone else. Individuality is a vital factor.

In recent years, some classic examples of 'hero worship' have been Bjorn Borg, John McEnroe and Chris Evert, who all generated their fair share of lookalikes. Good players have many points in common, but McEnroe's serve is unique to him and Borg's releasing of his double-handed backhand was also unique to him.

There was a long list of male tennis players ready to follow in Borg's footsteps, but it did not occur. If you look at all the Swedes that are playing now, you will see that they all have individual styles. Borg certainly set the trend for the emergence of Swedish tennis, but players eventually realized that they had to develop their own type of play.

The same thing happened with Chris Evert. Her success caused the cult of the double-handed disciplined baseliners. Tracy Austin succeeded, but many others failed.

So, do everything in your own individual style. Make yourself the player to be emulated. Do not seek out unnecessarily a particular trait of a good player and apply it to your own game, thinking that it is going to work for you.

Personality

Your own personality will influence the way you play and will overall be reflected in your game – although there are exceptions to the rule.

If you are an extroverted, outgoing sort of person, the odds are that you will try and play aggressive, attacking tennis. If you are an introverted, careful sort of person, you will probably play

Fig 117 Sabatini proved the critics wrong in winning the 1990 US Open. She worked hard on developing her personality to become more outgoing and positive.

Fig 118   Happiness is nine Wimbledon titles for Martina. Will this record ever be beaten?

a sensible, backcourt percentage game.

The introvert will rarely have a temper and will generally be patient and philosophical. He is often tactically astute and can make the most of any opportunity. The extrovert will probably be vulnerable to losing his temper, and his style of play will lean towards attack and more risk-taking.

Be aware that the way you are can reflect your style of play on the court. I have often felt, watching certain players, that their style does not quite reflect their personality, which creates inner conflict.

Certain players can take risk after risk after risk and not be perturbed by any mistakes that occur, while others can make a couple of very elementary errors, and then become extremely cautious when they should be looking to be positive and aggressive.

So if you are just beginning to play the game, be conscious of what style will best suit your personality.

Discipline

Sometimes, the natural player finds it difficult to accept that some of the problems within his game might be of his own making. He is looking for outside agents to blame in certain situations, whereas the method player – because of all the hours spent drilling and working hard – seems to be mentally tougher on the big points, almost craving for a crisis situation. In general, he is more able to cope with the problems – the bad line calls, the lucky bounces – than the more flamboyant player.

When it comes to the bottom line, when the pressure is on in match play, this is one key

point which can influence the outcome of the match. Overall, the disciplined style of player has the edge in this department over the more natural player. (Obviously, McEnroe, Nastase and Mandlikova have achieved an enormous amount, but how many more wins could they have tucked under their belt with a greater discipline in their game?)

However, the tendency towards mental fragility for flamboyant players is not inevitable, and providing they really want to go to the highest level, there is no doubt that they can use their talents more effectively.

Never Be Satisfied

To maximize your full potential, you should always be seeking out new ideas – in some cases to keep ahead of

129

Discipline

The prime exponent of discipline in recent years is Martina Navratilova. By developing a greater mental discipline, she has certainly encouraged a definite change in her character.

In her late teens and early twenties, Martina was a frustrated individual. She found it difficult to come to terms with her talent and was often seen to lose tight matches in despair. She was overweight and lacked discipline both in her game and her lifestyle.

Then, she took a long, honest look at herself and asked whether she was going to fulfil her potential. She realized that she would not, unless she made considerable changes, and she therefore sought out the help of dieticians and trainers – achieving probably more than she thought was possible from the game.

She has harnessed a great sliced backhand, she uses her topspin at the right times and has also simplified her game. She has taken out a lot of her fancy shots, but has retained the ability to use them as weapons whenever required. Her efforts, in turn, have inspired a new generation to seek out even higher levels of performance.

So, it can be done, but it requires some tremendous mental effort, much heartache, months and years of dedication and the ability to be totally honest with yourself at all times.

Fig 119   Martina Navratilova, who changed her ways to become an all-time great.

your rivals, and in other cases to make up lost ground.

You should therefore be monitoring your nearest rivals' performances extremely closely to pick up ideas which will help you develop new tactics.

For example, when Martina Navratilova made her move, Chris Evert knew that if she was to stay in touch with the rapidly improving Martina, she would have to look towards changing certain aspects of her game. She undoubtedly became more positive. She certainly took more risks and began to attack the ball more.

Ironically, those changes meant that she began to lose to players who had never beaten her before because of the supreme solidity and consistency of her game. But to stay with Navratilova, she had to develop a more aggressive game and the gamble eventually paid off.

PART 3
DRILLS AND EXERCISES

14

PRACTISING

A very important factor in the teaching of tennis is the value of practice once the lesson is over. Many players are guilty of having a lesson and almost expecting a magical remedy to their problems.

Over the years, most of the players I have taught at all levels have benefited from sensible practice, that is, well-organized drilling. You will discover, especially with the better players, that particular drills are valuable in ironing out their weaknesses.

The best way to go about proper practice is to find yourself a partner of similar standard, who is equally keen to improve, and spend hours out sweating and toiling on the practice court.

There are many sensible ways for players of all levels to work on their game with a series of drills and exercises. The great thing about drilling is that it can be fun. But remember not to spend too much time on one particular drill, since boredom can easily set in and have a disruptive influence. Quality of practice, rather than quantity, is what really matters. A maximum of 15 minutes on any one drill is therefore ideal, unless, of course, it is being played for points, in which case you should play to the end of that particular session.

Rallying

Let us start. You are two players who have just started to develop your game, and the simplest of drills is learning to rally.

You should think in terms of setting yourselves goals. If you are capable of directing the ball over the net ten times, then, realistically, you should set yourselves a target of twenty.

That is the first aim of learning to drill – a twenty-stroke rally, chasing and returning the ball on one bounce each time. If you find it difficult to keep a rally going within the confines of the court, chase the ball wherever it goes so that you become accustomed to the habit of pursuing the ball. When the 20-stroke rally has been attained, increase the target to 30, then to 40 and so on, but keep it realistic.

Each time you go onto the court to play sets or points, you should first attempt a longer rally. By the time you are achieving 50- and 100-shot rallies, you are at the stage where you can develop your play. (At this time, I would strongly recommend trying to maintain a high quality of shot during the rally.)

As you progress, the next facet of rallying is to give yourselves higher-level objectives, which include seeking to hit the ball in a more confined area.

For example, you can put down hoops or ball cans in certain areas of the court and use them as targets. The most common drill – and this is even practised by the better players who may be struggling with their groundstrokes – is to put targets within 60–90cm (2–3ft) of the baseline and inside tramline and think in terms of rallying while aiming at the targeted areas. It is important here to stress that it is not just hitting to the target that is foremost, but at all times moving the feet to take the ball on one bounce. It is also important to keep the rally going.

As your playing standard improves and you develop the feeling of the rally, the rally should cease when the ball is out of play (i.e. when it has bounced twice, or outside the lines). Obviously, you can try hitting down the lines or cross-court, but keep up the quality of the rallies by maintaining speed and weight of shot. Make sure at all times that boredom does not creep in and that there is a feeling of concentration and application to the task.

As you begin to improve, you will become aware of the importance of being able to direct the ball deep, close to the baseline. An excellent drill is to think in terms of rallying, with targets of 30, 50, 100 or whatever you think you are capable of doing – and making sure the ball lands between the service line and the baseline. If the ball is short of the service line or over the baseline, then the rally ceases. It is a great exercise to improve your ability to play to length. I have also seen some fine players who compete at a high level bring in another line, between the service line and the baseline. They are aware of the need to improve their length so much that they put in the extra line so they are looking at a 1 or 1.5m (4 or 5ft) area.

So, you can experiment, adding an extra line at each end. It is of paramount importance to realize and appreciate the value of deep groundstrokes. Playing to a consistent length is one of the basic requirements to perform at a high level.

As we are discussing groundstroke skills, I think it is important to stress that at the beginning, according to the shape of shot that you have – whether it be topspin, slice or flat – you can do variations in all these drills. You can insist on slice only, topspin only, or on hitting your least favoured shot. This helps to improve your repertoire of shots and development and understanding of spin.

Variety is Essential

Obviously, all players have certain basics on which they will rely throughout their playing days, certain strengths which form the backbone of their game. Nevertheless, it is important for all players to work on a variety of less favoured aspects of their game in order that they become well-rounded.

Take, for example, a player who likes using his forehand; he should practise long rallies during which he can only play backhands. If he hits a forehand, then the rally ceases. This is a simple exercise which can be extended to different strokes. From here, we can examine other methods of practising and perfecting all the various skills. Let us look at a number of exercises, the first of which is as follows.

One player remains standing in one corner and plays the feeding role, hitting the ball from side to side. The other player is mobile and will run from side to side, returning the ball to the area where the 'feeder' is standing.

At an elementary level, I would suggest that both players work with the following format. The player in the feeding role will play three balls down the line, which the mobile player will hit back to the same area. On the fourth ball, the switch occurs when the player feeding hits the ball cross-court. The mobile player will respond by running along the baseline and returning the ball to the feeder who then hits three more balls cross-court and the next down the line. The exercise is then repeated until the rally breaks down. Three balls down the line, and then three balls cross-court.

You can now see the pattern of the drill, and if carried out diligently, it will teach accurate rallying and consistency. As the players' standard improves, the drill can be reduced to two balls each way and eventually to one ball in each direction. This exercise not only encourages accuracy, but is also valuable in promoting good footwork, recovery and stamina.

It is important that the person in the feeding role realizes that the quality of the feeding is essential if the exercise is to be worthwhile for his running partner.

As the mobile player begins to tire, feel he is losing interest or his mechanics are breaking down, he should switch roles

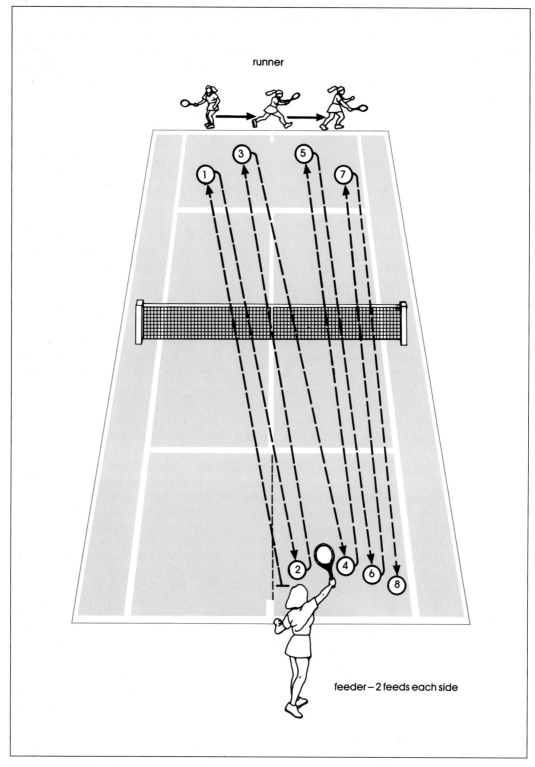

Fig 120   Two balls each way – keep the sequence going until the rally breaks down.

with his partner. However, it is imperative that he is made to understand the cause of the breakdown. If it is fatigue, he will obviously have to switch, but if it is loss of concentration, it would be wise to try and regain the earlier quality for a short period before switching roles.

You can also introduce some variety in this exercise, because the feeding role can obviously be played from the right- or the left-hand court.

This particular exercise is one that is used by many of the finest players. It enhances their security from the back of the court, teaches them the ability to run from side to side, and is also very good for introducing the *concentration* needed for long rallies.

Volley Exercises

So far, all we have dealt with are ground-stroke skills at a very elementary level. The next stage is learning about the volley.

I personally believe that the simplest method of encouraging people to feel comfortable about their net position is to start with two players approximately 1.5 or 1.8m (5 or 6ft) from the net. The sole intention should be to keep the rally going very easily and comfortably without letting the ball touch the ground.

Often, when volleyers are learning about the net position, they are intimidated by the weight of shot from a ground-stroke. This is why, to build the confidence of the net player at an elementary stage, the players should be encouraged to volley to each other at a very sensible speed. They are not in competition at this stage. Again, I would suggest that they try to rally to certain targets – 20, 30, 40 and so on – to make them feel at home in the net position.

The following exercise is one which has proved very successful over the years.

Both the net players stand outside the service line (i.e. between the service line and the baseline). Neither player is allowed to touch the area between the service line

and the net. Again, the aim is to not let the ball touch the playing surface.

This is a difficult exercise which is very demanding on the wrists and forearms, but it will promote greater depth and feel for the volleyers. If you are capable of doing a 40- or 50-stroke rally in this way, you will be in a position to approach the net with a high degree of confidence.

Another area which will improve your net game is if you alternate between forehand and backhand – again, setting yourselves sensible targets.

Once you feel able to carry out a sensible rally, it is probably worth creating a situation between a volleyer and a groundstroker.

An excellent exercise for learning to control the volley to a good length is where the volleyer tries to strike the ball between the service line and the baseline. It also requires good control from the baseliner if you are going to achieve rallies of 30 strokes or more.

The Overhead

Many people ask me for an exercise to improve their overhead shot. The following exercise requires approximately twenty balls.

The backcourt player will act as the feeder. There will be no rallying in this exercise. The net player takes up his ready position, waiting for the groundstroker to feed him a lob overhead. As soon as the ball is fed, the net player responds by moving back and executing an overhead or smash, after which he runs forward and touches the net. Immediately he touches the net, another lob is fed from the groundstroker, so the net player moves back again to make another smash. The routine is continued in this way until the twenty balls are exhausted.

It is a tiring exercise, but one which will certainly reap its rewards. The feeder

Fig 121   Yannick Noah displays fine athleticism on the overhead.

should always be using a single ball, and there should be no attempt to keep the rally going.

The following routine is to give the net player the confidence to integrate the volley and the smash.

Exactly the same process is used, starting with twenty balls. Instead of waiting for the player to run in and touch the net, the ball is fed out encouragingly for him to volley. By 'encouragingly', I mean that the feed is there to help the net player, and not to try and beat him.

This exercise is important in developing the skill of hitting a volley while on the move, which is so essential to the first volley behind the serve and to the recovery volley after executing the smash.

Complete the sequence by using all twenty balls, alternating between a smash and a volley. Again I must stress that the point is not to keep the rally going, but to feed each ball individually.

Too often when people are practising these drills, only the person who is involved in doing a particular exercise seems to concentrate. It is just as vital for the feeder to always apply himself, because if the feeding is not right, the participants are simply not going to maximize the benefit of these drills.

One word of warning: ensure that there are no loose balls on the net player's side of the court which could cause him to trip over.

The Serve

Many people fail to practise their service enough. How often have you seen players waiting around at clubs for a partner, while the courts are free and all they need is a plentiful supply of balls?

If you visit any tournaments on the professional circuit, you will notice that there are always players practising their serve. The value of the serve is enormous and is the only stroke over which the player has complete control. It initiates each game and, after all, you do have to serve every other game in singles. It simply cannot be avoided.

Many areas of one's game can be protected – covered up – but a weak serve will always be vulnerable. Some players who are limited in certain aspects of their game nevertheless manage to develop a fine serve which enables them to play at a level they probably would not have been able to achieve otherwise.

Just think of Barbara Potter and Roscoe Tanner. Both worked tremendously hard on their service game, more so than on any other shot. Both carried around a bag of balls and some old ball cans which were used as targets, and both could be seen out on the practice court for hours at a time, developing their serve into a potent weapon.

When a player is trying to develop his serve it is imperative that he does not only practise pace but also positioning. Many of the players on tour who practise their serve will put targets in strategic positions on the court to help them develop variety in their serve, to include sliced serves, flat serves, topspin serves and kick serves.

Linking Mind and Body

I am often asked about exercises which help make the feet and mind respond more swiftly and in unison with each other.

One exercise, which I believe to be very useful and worth watching good players perform, begins when two players feed the ball to each other at a sensible pace from the back of the court. If the ball is going to their forehand, they must move to play a backhand; likewise, if the ball is going to their backhand, they must move to play a forehand. It requires a lot of energy, but it improves footwork and makes you think very quickly. Remember, however, that it must be done at a sensible pace, otherwise the drill is impossible to put into effect.

The following is another good exercise, which helps develop two areas for the backcourt player. It promotes good footwork, and the confidence for the player to trust both of his groundstroke wings.

Within the rallies, the aim is for each player to hit a forehand, followed by a backhand, then a forehand, and so on until the pattern breaks down and the rally obviously ceases.

This exercise can also be linked to set rally targets – 30, 40, 50 and so on. If players can reach 100 or 150, they are certainly ready to grace a court and play competitive tennis, even if it be at club level. When you reach this level of consistency, you can add some fun to the exercise by raising the quality of the rallies.

Many players become frightened of attacking the ball, and this can even apply at the highest level. One possible method to help the player out of this crisis is to put the onus on attack 'by command'. By this, I mean that you could create a rally situation where the player, on the command of 'NOW!' from the feeder, has to go for a winner.

The benefit of this exercise is that for a period of time it forces the player to attack, and eventually – with diligent practice – it can bring back lost confidence in that area of the game.

Elevation

Another important area is learning how to move and play with elevation.

Elevation is an essential factor in being able to recover your position, while at the same time completing the stroke and maintaining good balance in order to be ready to play the next shot. It is achieved by naturally allowing the weight transference to almost lift you off the ground while executing the shot.

Notice how the majority of the top players today are hitting a large percentage of their shots with their feet off the ground.

Elevation is now a vital ingredient of the

Fig 122   Michael Chang showing good elevation while taking an early ball.

modern game. This means that top players have had to become highly mobile athletes, sacrificing the classic finish to their stroke production which used to be a normal part of the game.

Having had the privilege of following the professional tour and working with Jo Durie, I can venture to say that the finest tennis players in the world are capable of playing their shots in any situation, with the ability to use elevation, as a routine part of their game.

Once you feel comfortable using elevation within the formation of your strokes, you will note much more fluency in your game. Remember, do not consciously lift your feet off the ground to create elevation. Allow it to occur naturally through the transference of weight into your shot.

Let us create an exercise. Again, its effectiveness will depend on the accuracy and consistency of the feeder. The drill will be practised in a twosome.

Fig 123   Here is an excellent example of elevation, with Jo showing how she can gain extra power by using the legs to propel herself into the ball. Notice how Jo is still balanced and controlled while playing the shot.

Figs 124 and 125   Forehand and backhand running drives. Both these sequences demonstrate the difficulty of playing the ball on the run. Despite being obviously stretched, note the balance and poise shown during the shot. To compete successfully at tennis, you must be able to hit the ball on the run.

Create a drill in which one shot is played off the back foot, the next shot off the front foot and the next shot with both feet off the ground. Meanwhile, the feeder keeps striking the ball back as evenly and as comfortably as he can. This exercise gives the player the facility to play without the preoccupation of searching for the so-called perfect technique. It has certainly worked

wonders with several of my players, in making them appreciate that they can learn to play the ball from any position.

As with the other exercises, this should be done for about 10–15 minutes. Then, player and feeder can switch roles and keep the same pattern going – front foot, back foot, both feet off the ground – no matter what shot comes the player's way.

Fig 125

Points Within Drills

So far, I have only suggested drills for the benefit of the player seeking to develop his skills, consistency and stamina.

The natural follow-on is to devise drills where you play for points, and that changes the direction of the practice sessions. Playing for points makes you less methodical, and introduces the fun element of competition.

Before we discuss any particular exercises, I would suggest that you arrange to play the points to 11, 15 or 21, depending on how long you wish to spend on the exercise. Remember, the emphasis is on fun, but at the same time you should be encouraging the competitive aspect of the

141

runner

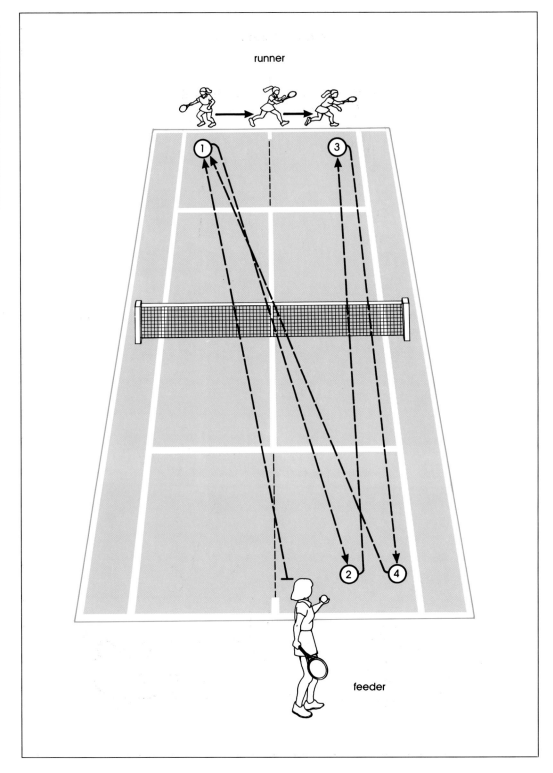

feeder

Fig 126   One ball each way – continue in this pattern until the point is won.

both run – 1 shot each way

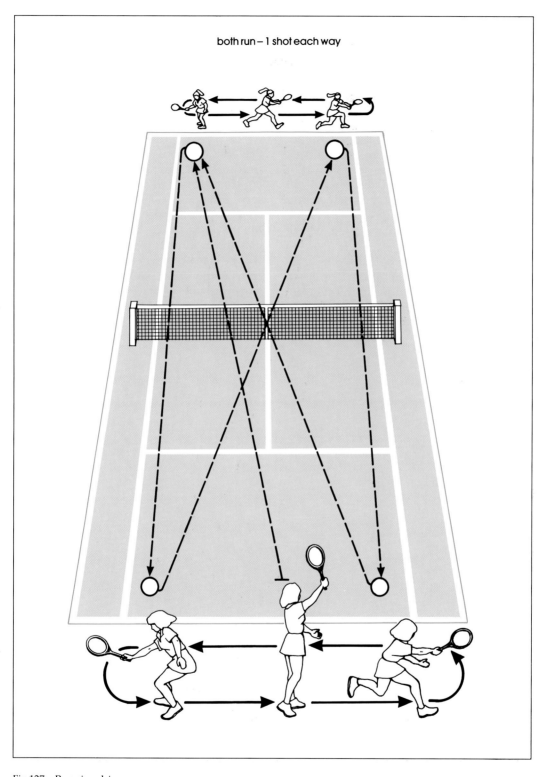

Fig 127 Running drives.

game. And now, let's turn our attention to the exercises.

One player is standing still, the other running. The player who is standing still has to hit the ball into the singles court between the centre service line and the left tramline. His next shot then has to go between the centre service line and the right tramline. The receiver must always hit the ball back to the forehand part of the court only. On completion of the exercise, the players will switch roles (*see* Fig 126). Obviously, if you wish, you can also repeat exactly the same exercise from the backhand side of the court.

The next stage is for both players to be running, but one has to hit the ball down the line while the other has to hit it cross-court. This will then create a pattern of down the line/cross-court, down-the-line/cross-court (*see* Fig 127).

It will become apparent that the likely winner, if both players play approximately to the same standard, will be the one who plays cross-court. It really is an achievement if you manage to win this exercise while only playing the ball down the line.

Players of a more advanced level can add another dimension to this drill by specifying that every ball must land beyond the service line. If it falls short of the service line area, the point is lost. This really does force the player to realize the need to be able to play his groundstrokes to length, and you will be hard-pressed to find a more difficult, competitive situation. Any tennis player capable of playing this exercise well is at a very fine level indeed.

15

HALF-COURT EXERCISES

On many occasions, when players arrive to play singles at the club, they are reluctantly forced into playing doubles because of the demand for courts. One possibility is that if all four players would like to practise for their singles game, they can use some of the following half-court exercises.

In all half-court exercises, tramlines will be included in the area of play. Again, you can play the games up to 11, 15 or 21 points.

Playing to Length

The first exercise (*see* Fig 128) is used to encourage the volleyer to play to length. Throughout the whole of the game, the volleyer will start the rally off. Every volley has to go between the service line and the baseline. If the balls falls short of that area, the point is lost. The restriction on the groundstroker is that he is not allowed to lob at any time. This will naturally improve his repertoire of passing shots and his ability to dink.

A follow-on exercise from this is where any shot is allowed by either the volleyer or the groundstroker. The only restriction is that the first feed from the volleyer cannot be a stop volley. He has to feed the ball to length and only then can the full range of shots be played by either player.

The 'Smash Game'

This exercise encourages the net player to have more confidence in his overhead.

At the outset, the smasher can stand no further back than the service line. It is

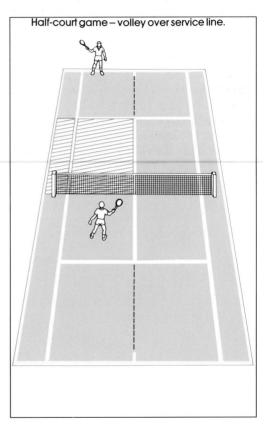

Half-court game – volley over service line.

Fig 128   Half-court game – volley over the service line.

compulsory for the groundstroker to feed the first stroke of the rally as a lob. As the ball leaves the groundstroker's racquet, the smasher can move to any part of his playing area in preparation of making his shot.

There are two variations of this game. In the first, it is compulsory after making the smash to go forward in order to make a volley, whereas in the other variation the smasher – if he so wishes – can hit a groundstroke before going to the net again.

Fig 129 Jennifer Capriati has based her success on a solid backcourt game. However, she is more than capable of putting away the volley.

These exercises are both excellent for improving the smash and for backcourt players to learn to get back into the rally after receiving the smash.

Winning from the Net

This is one of the best half-court exercises. The volleyer always feeds the first ball to a sensible length. The rally then proceeds with either player allowed to hit any type of shot they wish (drop shot, lob, dink, etc) until the point is decided.

If the net player wins the rally, the score becomes 1–0 in his favour and he retains the net position. If he has lost the point, the score remains at 0–0. They then switch roles and the net player becomes the groundstroker.

It is apparent that the only way to win is by retaining the net position. The exercise will therefore encourage all players to learn to win from the net.

16
PLAYING SETS

Generally speaking, most players at all levels have certain aspects of their game which they would like to improve within the framework of match play – hence the value of playing practice sets. Unfortunately, so many players are afraid of losing points even in practice situations that they become frightened of experimenting and trying out new ideas. A more positive approach should therefore be encouraged.

An obvious way of improving your ability within sets is by playing against a variety of opponents who all have different styles of play. Some of the following variations on how to play sets could help you overcome some fears over certain aspects of your game.

For example, if two players are very solid and reliable from the back of the court and they both want to develop their net game, they should play some sets where it is compulsory to serve and volley – perhaps in the beginning on the first serve only, and then as they gain confidence, on both serves.

Another good variation on playing sets is to make it compulsory to have only one serve. This will really develop your second service, in as much as you will have to play a 'safe' serve.

Players who are trying to improve on their length can play sets in which every ball has to go beyond the service line – except, naturally, the serve.

Another variation, and in my experience one that can be a lot of fun, is to ban the volley. By that, I mean that if you can make your opponent play a volley, then your opponent loses the point. It tends to encourage players to try drop shots and angles to bring the opponent into the vulnerable area, where a volley can be forced. This exercise naturally changes the way players would think about strategy, and encourages them to try for the 'feel' shots, the ones which require delicate control – the touch shots.

Another exercise which encourages players to be more positive, is when the server is compelled to go for a winner on or before his fourth stroke of the point. This makes the server seek out winning opportunities on the court, while the receiver is placed in a more defensive role, running the ball down probably more than usual because he knows that if the rally goes beyond 8 shots, he will win the point.

When you are striving to learn the approach shot, you should play sets where it is compulsory that every time the ball lands in the service box area, you have to go forward and make an approach shot to attack from the net position. On occasions, you will be forced into a difficult situation, but overall this variation encourages you to seek the opportunity to go in to the net as much as possible.

During practice sets, use the time to develop areas of your game in which you are relatively weak or lack confidence. I am not suggesting that you change your whole way of playing, but the more comfortable you feel in the areas where you know you are weak, the more confidence you will gain, the less you will panic when crisis situations occur in matches.

Prior to playing sets, players must bal-

Fig 130   Agassi – a perfect example of early preparation on the backhand.

ance out and decide which particular object they have in mind. Too many players get paranoid in practice sets if they are struggling to perform to the level they would like to attain.

Many of the best juniors I have seen around in recent years become very agitated if they cannot win their practice sets. Obviously, they should be playing their sets positively, but if they are seeking to improve and develop their game, they should accept defeat with a critical, but philosophical and constructive outlook.

More players would be able to develop their game if they stopped being so competitive in practice sets and started to use them for what they are: a means to improve their skills. Let them save their will to win

purely for their matches, when, hopefully, they can bring into use some of the skills on which they have been working.

To be able to play effective, winning tennis at a competitive level, you have to learn to develop many aspects of your game. You should therefore learn to relax when playing practice sets – too much anxiety over winning will prevent the necessary development in the many areas that need to be improved. Short term sacrifice is for long term gain.

Your ultimate aim is to fulfil your potential, but please be aware that, in some cases, over-keenness and the desire to win can be detrimental to the long term well-being of your game.

17
EXTRA TIPS

Improving Reactions

I am often asked about how a pupil can learn to improve his reaction time and how he can see the direction of the ball sooner. This is an extremely difficult area, but here are a couple of exercises which might be of use.

In the first one, the feeder has a basket of balls and each ball is fed individually from the net. (Keeping a rally going is not the object of the exercise.)

The receiver stands in an orthodox position on the baseline and actually closes his eyes. When the feeder is about to strike the ball, he calls 'NOW!' The receiver then responds by opening his eyes and trying to pick up the flight of the ball.

This is a very interesting exercise, because often a lot of players panic initially – although they do become far more perceptive and their reaction time improves considerably as the drill progresses. What appeared difficult at the beginning will, within 15 minutes appear to be a very easy feed. Because the player's eyes are closed, he becomes far more eager and much more perceptive and will start to look for and pick up the flight of the ball much more keenly.

A follow-up exercise is to make the receiver turn round and face the back fence and, using the same idea, the feeder shouts 'NOW!' as he is about to strike the feed. It is interesting to see how slowly the player responds at the beginning, but with practice and as time goes by, he will definitely become more reactive and keener to chase the ball.

This exercise does require some precise feeding and a knowledge of how well the receiver can move. It is pointless to feed out balls that are impossible to return, but as time goes on, the participants will develop a much more instinctive ability to pick up the flight of the ball.

Naturally, this exercise can be carried out from the back of the court, where the feeding originates from the baseline and you will be working on developing the net player's reaction. It is surprising how quickly the first reflex on the volley can be improved.

The Delicate Shots

Players often want exercises to practise the 'feel' shots – the touch volleys, the stop shots, the half volleys (*see* Fig 131).

There is one drill which when practised involves all three of these particular shots. Several top players often use this drill to warm up very gently at the beginning of their practice sessions. However, I personally feel that the best way to gain from the following exercises is to play them competitively – but not aggressively. Play them for points – the first to 11, 15 or 21 and so on. The drill is intended to develop quick reactions and to encourage the 'feel' shots (i.e. the ones that require delicate racquet control).

Quite simply, the service areas become the playing zones. If the rallies progress to 10 or 15 shots you will be surprised how tiring the drill can become, because of the dimensions of the service box area. As you are having to work in such a confined area, it becomes more like a squash game and extremely demanding.

Fig 131   McEnroe at his best, showing fine skill in playing a delicate stop volley.

Fig 132 Who better than McEnroe for touch and finesse?

One or two variations can be found within the framework of the drills. The easiest one to start with is to play from one service box to the opposite service box (*see* Fig 133). Then, you progress to playing the diagonals either way (*see* Fig 134), and then to covering the whole of the service box area (*see* Fig 135).

Due to the dimensions of the playing area, the serving will always be with an under-arm feed.

This is obviously a good exercise for a backcourt player who wishes to develop his forecourt game, and the nature of the drill means that it is not only an exercise for developing the touch shots, but it can also be used for light relief. It becomes apparent that the only way to win points is to out-manoeuvre the other player, and this is where the sense of fun comes into the game.

Changes of Spin and Pace

During match play certain players are vulnerable to changes of tactics by the opposition – slow balls for instance, or opponents suddenly using more topspin.

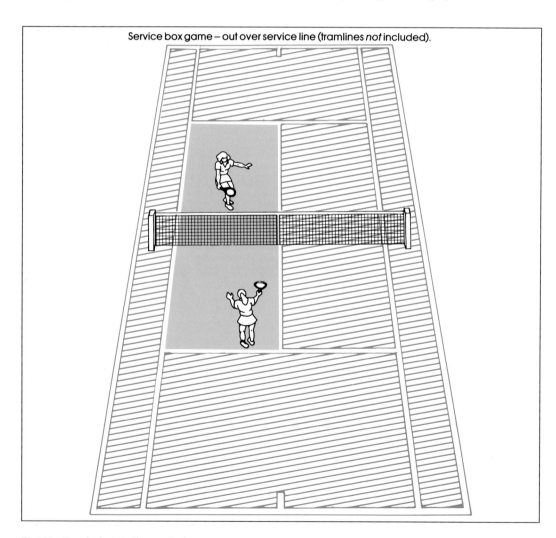

Service box game – out over service line (tramlines *not* included).

Fig 133   Touch shots in the service box.

Here again, I am assuming a high level of integrity in the two players practising with each other. The feeder has to be very diligent and precise in his role.

Both players will set up a backcourt rallying situation, in which neither will be trying to out-gun the other. They will just rally at a sensible pace. As the rally is progressing, the feeder will be in command and insist that his colleague plays topspin. A little later, he will demand slice, for instance. So the rally continues with the feeder demanding a change every so often.

Several commands can be used. These are: topspin, slice, flat and the moonball (hitting the ball very high). Alternatively, the feeder could demand that his partner become notably more aggressive.

Since many players get rutted into one way of playing, this is an excellent exercise to encourage them to experiment with other areas of the game.

As you develop your repertoire of spins and tactical changes, such as slow-balling, you will also learn to recognize such tactics in your opponent's game.

Remember this. Practice does not make perfect. Perfect practice makes perfect. Far too many players do not use their practice

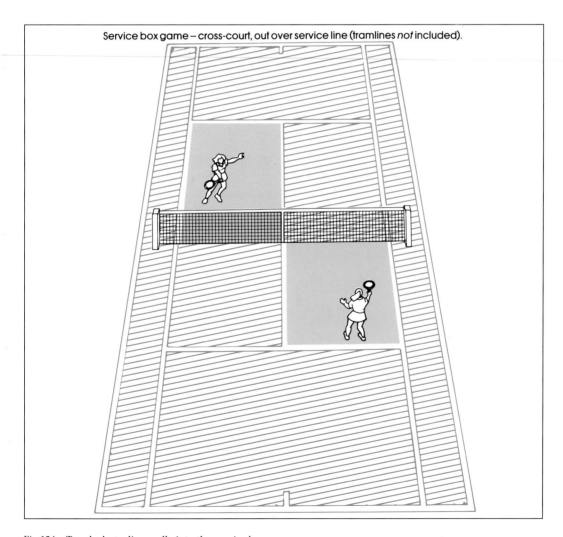

Fig 134   Touch shots diagonally into the service box.

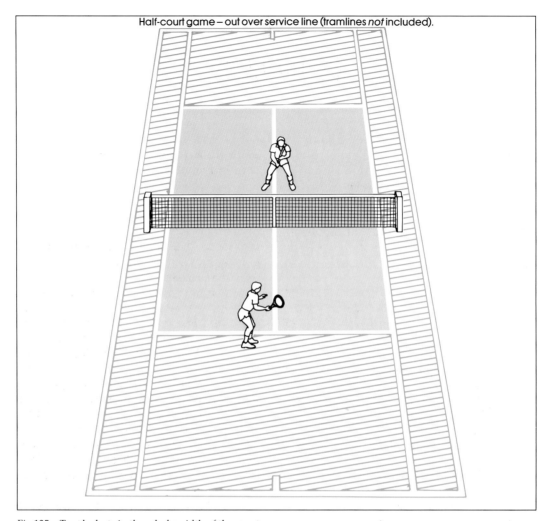

Half-court game – out over service line (tramlines *not* included).

Fig 135   Touch shots in the whole width of the court.

sessions properly. If you can at least develop sensible practice sessions you will reap the rewards.

The more you can chase the tennis ball, the more you will develop the physical side of your game and improve muscle strength and stamina. The majority of the top players believe that most of their physical work is done on the court by chasing the ball. There is no other real substitute than this for improving your fitness and athleticism.

18
EQUIPMENT

Ball Baskets

Ball baskets can be invaluable. From the absolute beginner to the professional player, benefits can be gained from using them.

Most ball hoppers carry about fifty balls. Rallies will not be played when using the basket since the drilling is dependent on single feeds.

Obviously, the degree of feeding – use of tempo, width, pace of shot – will create the level of pressure under which the player will be and, naturally, the beginner will require easier feeding than the expert.

Although the exercise is dependent on the individual feed, in essence, we are still creating a 50-stroke rally, because the ball is being fed continuously.

The Americans seem the keenest users of the basket and I can recall Tracy Austin and Chris Evert in their early days spending endless hours working with them.

This type of practice encourages the back-court player to improve his discipline, by feeding the ball consistently from side to side. It will encourage the player to improve his passing shots and, according to where the feeder stands with the basket, angles can be created as a means to experiment.

In the same vein, the net player can improve and develop his game by a feeder using a ball basket from the baseline. It is certainly an area in which players can improve not only their technique but also their stamina, speed and reactions if the ball is fed under severe pressure.

The mental discipline required to carry out consistent drilling with the baskets needs to be of the highest calibre. Two of the world's most famous tennis academies, Nick Bollettieri's and Harry Hopman's – both based in Florida – include the basket routines as a large part of their training programme.

Ball Machines

What can you do if you cannot find a playing partner or a coach? You could try the ball machine.

The ball machine has been very much a part of the American way of life for years. However, many of the larger clubs in the UK are now able to offer the use of a machine. It provides a regular, constant feed and can be set to feed the ball at a variety of speeds, angles, heights and rhythms. If you are looking to groove your groundstrokes; the ball machine is your answer. For best results, it is worth putting in good quality balls, because poor quality ones will not filter through particularly well. Most ball machines will take between forty and sixty balls.

I would readily recommend the use of machines for beginners and also for players making a comeback from injury, because they can spend hours grooving their shots again, while not needing to run around the court. They do not even need their coach there.

Another great aspect of the machine is that it can be a useful tool if you are going through a period in which you are struggling with your game and lacking confidence. Since it gives you a regular feed and a regular bounce, it will allow you to groove your strokes so that you can iron out those little kinks that have developed under the hazardous pressure of match play. Used sensibly and imaginatively, it can give you hours of pleasure as well as being a useful working tool.

Fig 136   Playing on your own, against a practice wall or ball machine, enables you to concentrate on a particular stroke and to groove it.

The Practice Wall

Many clubs have a practice wall. It can be ideal for warming up and getting accustomed to the feeling of strings on the ball.

The greatest asset of the wall is that it never misses, thus enabling you to obtain a constant rhythm. The wall is probably most beneficial for helping to improve the volley.

19
'THREES'

So far, we have discussed exercises between two players to improve their game during practice. One of the most commonly used methods the tour professionals employ is an exercise termed 'threes'.

As the name suggests, it will always involve three players. It is used by all the finest players in their practice sessions and it requires a high level of intense and demanding work. 'Threes' cannot be shirked by players if they are going to achieve at the highest level.

There are many variations within the terminology of 'threes'. Some require a quick turnover rate – by that, I mean that the work rate is so intense that the player in the physically active role will be unable to sustain his efforts for more than 1 or 2 minutes at a time. Other 'threes' will be structured around longer periods and can go on for several minutes.

'Threes' builds up concentration, stamina, fitness, strength and speed.

The general idea is to create intense pressure and teach the player to sustain rallies under those circumstances. Such pressure will rarely occur in actual matches, which consequently will often appear comparatively easy. Again, the value of the feeding role is absolutely vital. Essentially, the idea is for two of the three people to play the ball around, so that the other individual has to work very hard.

A large number of balls are required, so that even if one ball is missed, there is always another for a quick feed. With such a large number of balls used in these exercises it is inevitable that some will stray onto the court. Please be aware of this danger and clear them away at the earliest opportunity.

Generally you will find that the very fast, hectic 'threes' takes place when two of the three players volley at the net and the person at the other end fervently chases each ball. Always be aware that he must retrieve the ball after one bounce only. The feeders are trying to play the ball around in such a way that it creates pressure on the player. They should not try for winners, but continually place the ball in different and sometimes awkward places.

Because such an intense situation is created, as soon as the individual feels that he is losing strength in his movements, or that his technique is breaking down, it is imperative that he stops, otherwise he will cease to gain from the exercise. Always keep that point in mind when playing 'threes' at this level. As soon as tiredness sets in, one of the feeders should take over the player's role and the player become a feeder.

Many variations exist on this exercise. Although the basic idea of 'threes' is to encourage players to respond to intense pressure – which, in itself, creates tough physical sessions – 'threes' can be tempered for accuracy and consistency. One major weakness area is the loss of direction that occurs in making shots under pressure, so several of the following exercises aim to combat this.

'Threes' for Backcourt Play

One exercise is to make it compulsory to alternate each shot to the feeders, so that even under intense pressure, the mobile player is still thinking in terms of trying to impart some direction on the ball. You can also set up a situation where a 50-stroke rally has to be performed. The exercise

157

Yet another variation is to put a 10-minute time limit on the exercises, which would normally require the feeders to play the ball at a sensible tempo. I can assure you that those 10 minutes can seem like a lifetime, but the benefit in application of concentration and improved stamina is well worth it.

'Threes' for the Net

Probably the quickest and most demanding exercises occur when the two feeders are at the back and the player is at the net.

The first method can be described as 'anything goes'. The feeders can lob, drive, dink, apply pressure in any way they see fit; and that is hell!

An extremely difficult variation is for the net player not to let the ball touch the ground.

Still another is to insist on the net player playing smash and volley in that sequence throughout the 'threes'.

One of the finest aspects of a good net player is the ability to jump almost goalkeeper-like while playing the high-floating ball, and to encourage that type of skill, the feeders will have to apply themselves to provide a high level of accuracy in their feeding.

Developing Weight of Shot

One drill that is often used by the players on the professional tour is very beneficial in this area.

The exercise requires both parties to work from the baseline and to strike the ball to and fro at a sensible length. The individual player is looking to be more aggressive and on his fourth shot will attempt an attacking shot. The feeders, meanwhile, are simply playing a baseline rally, aiming to keep a steady pace. This exercise is obviously good for the feeders as well, because it creates the opportunity for them to react, chase and run down an attacking shot.

As far as possible, the rallies should be continuous. There are no points at stake, and this gives the player complete freedom with no inhibitions in how to strike the ball.

This drill can be changed by insisting that on every fourth strike the aggressor has to attack the net by means of an approach shot. This also provides another form of attack, since it forces the opposition to go for passing shots.

Naturally, the drill can be changed slightly by making the aggressor attack the ball on his third strike instead. This offers a useful variation.

PART 4
COACHING

COACHING

20

THE INITIAL APPROACH

The role of the coach varies according to the standard of the player or players with whom the coach is trying to work.

In my experience, tennis is a very difficult game to learn at the outset, both for adults and youngsters, and so very special training is required at that level.

Coaching players at an elementary level requires a special type of coach. A coach at that level needs to have patience, he needs a sense of humour, and he must have the ability to make people who find the game hard feel at ease on the court.

Almost everyone finds the game difficult at first and it is easy to become frustrated. The easiest course is to give up, and an overly demanding or unsympathetic coach may deter beginners from the game for ever. The beginner must be able to relax, gradually gain confidence on the court and enjoy the game as much as possible.

Professional players are often seen to suffer and agonize on the tennis court, but beginners should realize that it does not have to be that way all the time. Professionals are in a special situation, for with such high prize money and their livelihood at stake, it is perhaps understandable that they become emotional. They are doing a job, and as in any other job, there are moments of stress. Tennis is an intense business which demands a special mental attitude (see Part 5), but it must be imprinted on the beginner, and indeed anyone who wants to play, that tennis is first and foremost a game, and is there to be enjoyed. If all it does is lead to emotional problems, then perhaps it would be better to divert the player to other interests.

A good tennis coach is more than just a technical teacher. If he knows his job well, not ony is he developing technical skills but he should also be improving his pupil's mobility, stamina and strength. He should also be good at imparting psychological help and in helping concentration and developing a positive attitude and mental toughness.

There is no doubt that if a coach focuses exclusively on pure technique, then beginners will quickly lose interest. The object at the outset is to make the player relate to the tennis court and to the movement of the ball – which is the cause of many problems – and to focus exclusively on technical aspects of the game at such an early stage can be damaging to the pleasure of the pupil. There is plenty of time to build it into the game at a later stage.

The role of the coach at the initial stage is to supply information that makes the player feel at home on the court. Ball sense exercises of an elementary standard will be required and it is vital to be able to maintain the pupil's interest at this early stage, for instance, by ensuring that pupils gain a sense of achievement.

I have seen so many beginners feel terribly embarrassed at not being able to play the game. It is vital that tennis should be seen as fun at all times, and that beginners especially should not become tied up in technique and mechanics.

It is imperative that the coach stresses the value of movement. At all levels, tennis requires players to move and the dynamic Steffi Graf is an excellent example.

Since tennis is a moving game, I think the fun factor can be introduced by making the pupil aware of the ball and its flight. Teach your pupils that it is fun to achieve success by running for the ball and getting it back.

I encourage pupils not to worry about the court dimensions or the speed of the surface

Fig 138 Steffi Graf – arguably the fastest player in the women's game.

at this stage, but just to enjoy chasing the ball no matter where it is. Even if it is out, encourage them to get the ball.

Try to make them understand basic ball sense, to get the racquet on to the ball after one bounce time and time again, so that they build up a feeling for it. At the same time, they will learn that tennis is a very mobile sport. Let them have fun, and again do not get bogged down in technique.

Trust is Essential

It is essential, at any level, that the player learns to trust you.

There is no doubt that as a tennis player tries to develop and improve, the framework of his game will at some stage require changes, which may often be very difficult.

At an elementary and average level, a defensive method of play is generally more effective. However, as the transition from club level to tournament, to professional level occurs, so will the need for more aggressiveness linked to greater tactical skills and technique.

Naturally, to put the above process into effect, the player will have to make certain changes to his style of play.

If the player is already successful, it can mean that as the changes are made, his game will suffer at least a little in the short term. The aerobics cliché – no pain, no gain – applies equally to tennis.

So your role acquires an extra dimension. It is not soley geared to making the player improve – mutual respect must also come into it, so that the trust is there in difficult times.

You must be supportive. It is not easy to make changes – especially when the player already plays to a good standard – and to suffer the consequences until it eventually comes out right. It is difficult and frustrating to change a winning game and to convince the player it really is for the better.

But every player, from the beginner right up to the very best in the world, should never be satisfied with their game. There is always room for improvement or perhaps

for a new approach. You will never find Ivan Lendl or Steffi Graf resting on their laurels. They are out there on the practice court hour after hour, day after day, striving to polish or improve an already highly accomplished game.

You must share and understand the difficulties a player goes through at this time, and help him through it.

I have seen several top level players take a too short-sighted course, and maybe this is where pressure from the media and other outside agents is felt. Players have to keep faith in what they are doing. They must believe that the changes to their game are best in the long run, when people around them will be questioning their (temporarily) poor results.

Many times, players have been too frightened to experiment because of the pressures and demands that are placed on them. It can also be difficult for players of a high standard to recognize that their game has weak points that can be improved or eradicated.

It may hurt them psychologically, for there is always the temptation to tuck problems under the carpet and hope that the quality of the rest of their game will compensate for those weaknesses. I firmly believe, however, that the player who achieves the most is forever looking for ways to improve and develop.

Having said that, if you are working with a player who needs help, but is reluctant to accept that he does have problems, then that is where the trust factor comes in.

Visual Aids

The use of video is something that has come in over recent years. If a player seems to have an apparent weakness which he is reluctant to accept, then the great thing about video is that it does not lie.

The problem can be recorded, pointed out and explained, and it is far easier for the player to understand it by actually seeing it for himself. Once the problem is recognized, it is more difficult to hide away from it and deny it is there.

Fig 139   Ivan Lendl – a superb example of a highly dedicated professional.

Conversely, the video can be used as a form of positive reinforcement, showing a player how well he has performed in a certain area. Praise where it is due is a great stimulus and will bolster confidence on a bad day.

Exposing Weaknesses

Another way in which you can deal with a weakness is by exposing it with the help of other players.

Naturally some styles of play will cause problems to any individual and expose his vulnerability. I would bring in a player with that particular style and, within the practice session, require that player to set about attacking and exposing the weakness of the pupil.

One great asset of this method is that you can stop the exercise at any time and then discuss with your pupil how he can react and overcome the problem.

Sometimes, this method is not effective, because some players develop technical and mental blockages and feel uncomfortable working with other players. It is then your job to be out there, working relentlessly with the player, and to be forever homing in on the problem.

It is very easy to ignore a problem, but however painful or uncomfortable it may be, you must go to great lengths to make the player understand that all you want to do is help him. Your criticisms are only for the player's own good and to help him take a long-term look at himself. It is imperative that all players learn to look at their games honestly and responsibly, as this will lead them to become better tennis players.

Starting with a New Player

When starting work with a new player, I believe that within 20 or 30 minutes of play, a coach should have a very good idea of the standard that the pupil can attain.

Naturally, when working with a player

Over-Zealous Players

There are rare occasions where you might be working with an over-zealous player.

Isn't it ironic that while most of the time coaches in all spheres are stressing the need for work rate and dedication, every so often up pops an individual who is actually losing out by trying too hard?

This type of player requires a special kind of help, because from the coach's point of view it is always fun and rewarding to work with players who are giving their all. In this case, it is important to stress to the individual his long term goals, because if he cannot achieve his aims immediately, he often becomes frustrated and disillusioned. The over-zealous player is generally excitable and desperate for improvements to occur quickly and it is therefore important for the coach to make the pupil understand how to use surplus energy wisely and sensibly.

Trying to over-achieve can cause pressure in matches because the player becomes frustrated when he cannot deliver as well as he would like. This type of player can be a set up and with a point for 5–1, playing sensibly and intelligently and then, by playing one poor point, completely lose his direction by becoming over-anxious. Try and encourage this type of player to adopt a rational approach to the game and realize that every point is not a matter of life and death.

A good coach can be quite sneaky by playing this individual off against others who are lacking in motivation. The individual's attitude and work rate can often spur the others into performing better.

who is not so able, I strongly believe that it is up to the coach to make the player aware of his potential or lack of potential as early as possible. There is no point in stringing players along with false promises.

It is terribly important for players who are new to the game and just starting lessons to realize that only a small percentage of people playing tennis reach tournament standard, and therefore they should be realistic about their playing aspirations. That should help them to feel at home on the court and not expect too much of themselves, rather than be intimidated and worried about how dreadful they might appear.

When assessing a player at an early level you cannot think in terms of a Becker or a Navratilova. Often, when giving a private lesson, there will be plenty of club players – especially at weekends – to watch. Point them out to the pupil and give him confidence by explaining that most of those players out there were just like him at the beginning.

Beginners with natural ball sense and racquet co-ordination should be able to progress quickly, but with coaching, everybody should be able to reach a basic club standard.

Moreover, when assessing the pupil, never lose sight of the fact that the game is meant to be fun – the pleasure factor should always be there.

Do Not Outstay Your Welcome

Another important part of coaching is being aware that perhaps your time is up and that the relationship is not working anymore. Perhaps you have become so close to your pupil that you cannot see the wood for the trees.

I believe that working with a player is a two-way deal. The player may feel that it is time for a change of coach, and that is not easy if you are not prepared for this decision. You may feel that you still have more to offer. It may prove very difficult to recognize that your time is up, because all you can see is the success you have had with the player.

But there is more than one solution to every problem, and one coach may be able to see something that another misses. I have always believed that we should not be afraid to seek other people's advice. If someone makes a constructive observation about one of my players, then I am delighted. I think an exchange of ideas can only be beneficial.

I may have acquired a good store of knowledge, but I also know that I certainly do not have all the answers and therefore I always keep my ear to the ground. If you are prepared to keep listening and are receptive to comments and advice, then you will often learn a great deal.

I do not think there is any shame for a coach if his player wants to move on. One vital element of the pupil/coach relationship is being able to take a step back and imagine that you have never worked with this player before, so that you approach the situation with a fresh look.

It is a trick I use quite often. Sometimes, you can become so involved that you are oblivious to certain problems. If I have worked with a certain player over a long period of time and I am unhappy about the way things are going, then I treat the player as if he were a brand new pupil. I ignore the fact that I might have seen his forehand for the past eight years. It is a breath of fresh air for the mind – and it works. It helps me to look at areas that might have caused some frustration in the past and allows me to see any improvement or weaknesses.

It can also be quite healthy to take a break from a player for a couple of months, because when you see him again, it will be with new eyes and both you and the player will feel refreshed.

21
INTRODUCING TECHNIQUE

As players develop, seem to be comfortable in their movement and are becoming capable of producing rallies, the technical and mechanical factors of the game will have to be introduced.

There are obviously common factors which link the better players, however, there are certainly variations in style. It is therefore important to discover which way of playing best suits an individual.

For instance, a good young player may come to you with just a reasonable forehand. It is then your job to make him realize and appreciate that if he is going to progress in the long term, many other facets of his game will have to be developed in order that he may work his way up the ladder.

From my own experience, it is surprising how much reluctance there is to working on those areas. Good, young players tend to be strength-oriented, and you have to help them see that a clever opponent is going to play to their weaknesses and that ultimately, if they are going to improve, they must attempt to eradicate them. So, the earlier you can assist them, the better, and the less vulnerable they will feel playing at higher levels.

To some extent, the assessment of players is geared to the level at which they want to play. Pointing out weaknesses becomes far more important for the player at a competitive level than for the beginner.

Many youngsters get a little frightened of trying to develop their game in areas which, in the long term, will be of benefit to them. You have to be very encouraging and very convincing, and say: 'Hey, that's a good shot you have there, but watch out for those weaknesses. You will come up against better players who will expose them.'

Honest and critical assessment of a player who really does intend to make a go of tennis is vital.

Guidance

You have to recognize that youngsters can be so wrapped up in their need to win that they cannot see clearly enough how their game should develop for future years.

It is therefore up to you to have enough vision and confidence to look ahead for the benefit of your pupils. In my experience, many successful ten to fourteen year olds cannot develop into the senior game because they simply are not getting the right guidance.

Too many beginners are allowed to get away with areas of their game that cannot be developed to a high enough standard. Your role is to iron out those problems tactfully, but forcefully.

Motivation forms a major part of the coaching role and it is as important to the beginner as it is to the better player. Different things motivate different people and it is up to you to understand what motivates each individual pupil and to make it work.

If a player is going to be a success, he is going to have to spend a lot of time at dull areas of the game. During the monotony of drilling, the player's concentration will waver very easily.

Unless you can find ways to stimulate him, a player can just drift at this stage – although, ultimately, it is the player's self-motivation which will prove the critical factor, since you cannot always be there.

Discipline

Discipline is required with technique and in making a player get the best from himself. Discipline is also related to a player's attitude on court.

A player who knows the importance of raising his own game shows a great amount of discipline. Chris Evert and Bjorn Borg are two players who knew their game inside out. They were totally aware of what they had to do to get the best out of themselves.

So that is discipline – knowing not only how to play, but how to get the best out of your strokes at all times.

The player must also ensure that he has a good work rate. Plenty of people have queried what I exactly do mean by a good work rate, and my definition is: the ability to push oneself for long, intense periods without becoming physically or mentally sloppy.

That cannot come only from the coach, but also from within the player, and you can rest assured that all the top players have excellent work rates.

You cannot emphasize enough to the pupil that discipline in practice, technical development and work rate will pay ample dividends in the end.

Parents can often cause problems by becoming involved with this issue. Parents at all times should be supportive, both in defeat and victory, and they should be able to recognize that the player is competing for himself – not for the parents.

There are often two extreme approaches. On the one hand, we have the over-demanding parent who pushes his child to such an extent that the youngster ceases to derive any pleasure from the game. On the other, we have the parent who is far too protective and always trying to find excuses and reasons for little Johnny or Susie not making a proper effort.

In my experience, the majority of successful players have caring parents who properly balance the scales.

Remember that ultimately, if a pupil is

Fig 140   Chris Evert – an excellent tactician.

going to play tennis at the highest level and be an achiever, he will require a huge amount of self-motivation and single-mindedness, and that should be encouraged – not demanded – by the parents.

Motivation

To come through a crisis, through a long five-setter, a player will need a very tough mental outlook, and that can only be developed through discipline and self-motivation.

Motivation is often helped by change. Be aware of the possibility of boredom setting in and try to spot early on when it is time to change an exercise. Saturation point can be reached very quickly: be perceptive enough to know when a player has had enough and introduce a change in the routine or exercise. Mental stimulation is important, and it should be obvious when a player cannot handle the monotony of an exercise any more and it is time to call it a day.

For most players, the easiest way to gain motivation is through competition, and many an exercise can be used to that end. Often, if I am supervising a laborious drill and it becomes apparent that my pupils are losing concentration, I will change the exercise and get them to play a fun game where points are at stake. This will stimulate them into greater endeavour and re-kindle their appetite for work, such as a tough baseline rally.

You must be aware that it is not always easy for a player to be self-motivated. It is equally important for the player to know that if you are demanding more from him, then it is only for his own good.

Often, the most important factor in motivation is the self-satisfaction a pupil obtains from successful achievement. Encouragement and recognition from the coach also form a vital part of motivation, but other incentives can be used. One coach I know offers a free lesson if the player has worked especially hard. It is up to you to offer constructive advice and well-deserved rewards.

Fig 141 I think this is called motivating yourself!

Working Together

For a good coach/player relationship to be established, you must reassure the player that your efforts are geared to improving his game and that you will support him through thick and thin.

At some stage, the player's game – or part of it – might start going wrong, which will quite naturally induce disappointment and low spirits. This is where you must be at your most supportive – as long as, of course, the player is trying hard and is sincere in his efforts.

It is important that you make the player realize that he is going through a bad spell, and you must convince him that eventually, with some serious work, his form will return.

Even the great players suffer loss of form and poor performance spells. Ann Minter, one of Australia's top players is a good

Fig 142   A winning smile from Zina.

example. At one time, her serve broke down almost completely, but with the help of her coach and her own resilience she pulled herself out of it and went on to win a tournament. Never say die!

We can all motivate a player when he is up and things are going well for him. A sign of a good coach/player relationship is when things are going wrong and both parties are prepared to keep working to get things on the right track again.

The Coach in Match Situations

We have already discussed how the relationship between the coach and the pupil builds up on the practice courts. The ultimate test for both parties, however, is the contest on the match court.

On the professional circuit, on both the men's and women's tour, coaching from the sidelines is strictly forbidden. All the coaching should already have taken place

before the match, and it is the responsibility of the players to compete one on one. Naturally, but unfortunately, some players still attempt to communicate with their coaches. This is in breach of the rules, and in the first instance of being caught 'cheating' the player will receive a warning, which in turn could lead to disqualification if the offence is repeated.

However, in international team events, such as the Davis Cup, Federation Cup, Wightman Cup (*see* Fig 143) and so on, each team will have a non-playing captain who sits on court and is able to give guidance and direction at the change-overs. This is the nearest you will get to a player receiving coaching in the truest sense of the word during match play.

In this situation, the greatest asset that a captain must have is the ability to read the flow of the match and the emotions of the players concerned – not only of his own player but also of the opposition.

It is also vital, no matter what the crisis within the match, that the coach should not

Fig 143   Captain Virginia Wade assisting Jo Durie and Anne Hobbs in the Wightman Cup.

convey to his player any anxiety he might be feeling.

Coaching in match conditions requires a special talent in itself. You must judge the situation and decide whether, on some occasions, silence is better than words. In crisis situations, some players are happier left immersed in their own thoughts, and it is dangerous then to supply information, however relevant it may be.

Obviously though, if the player is struggling and nowhere near contention, it does no harm to put a little fire in his belly. If the match is very well balanced, then what you must not be seen to do is get excited, because that can often affect the way the player performs. Again, it is up to you to judge the situation and recognize the particular needs of each individual player.

Some obvious pointers that you can use can do very little damage. For instance, you could suggest that your player should be aware he is about to play a big game, and that between the points he should pause and take long, slow, deep breaths. Or simply that he should take his time and not rush. This type of observation will be seen by the player as supportive and will not confuse him.

Some players' game will really lift when a captain is on court. The psychological effect of a captain's presence helps in that the player may receive encouragement for his own tactical ideas, or talk over his doubts and receive moral support.

Essentially, your role is to be supportive, caring and not be seen to be stressed by the situation. At all times, it is vital that you bring an air of confidence to the proceedings and convey to the player a feeling of well-being.

Support from the Coach

We have discussed how a player can benefit from receiving advice during matches. However, such circumstances are rarely available and during the normal course of the professional's career, coaching is simply not allowed on court.

However, the support of a coach during match play is still extremely important in assisting the player with his performance.

You have to convey to the player that you are happy for him to be playing the match, no matter what the outcome. By this I mean that when the player looks towards you for some support in a match that he is losing, you should convey an attitude of support and not one of disappointment and frustration. No player wants to look up and see the coach with his head in his hands. The player should not feel pressure from the coach.

For instance, if a player has been working for several months on one aspect of his game, such as his serve, he may be worrying if it is not working properly. It is vital during the match that you are not seen to be dissecting every move that is made on the serve.

The player should just be getting on with the match. Afterwards, when the match is discussed, he should not feel uncomfortable towards the coach, even in defeat. Sometimes, after a match which a player feels he should have won, the best means of giving immediate help is to provide a shoulder to cry on.

It is imperative that the player understands that, come what may, he has practised to the best of his ability, and he is playing with whatever skills he has at his disposal at that particular time.

During matches, the player should be concentrating on his main objective – which is to perform to the best of his ability and hopefully win. He should not be worrying about what the coach is thinking or feeling.

One of the signs of a top class coach is that he has the ability to detach himself emotionally from his player's performance.

You cannot demand from your player that he should go out on court and play in a definite pattern, because once in the match the instincts of the individual take over. Also, the opposition may be able to suppress your pupil's game with their own strengths.

After matches, it is vital for the pupil to

feel that you are behind him, even if he has put in a bad performance. The judgement of the player after the battle can often be clouded, whilst you should have the ability to look clearly and long term at your pupil's performance.

It is very easy for a coach to get wrapped up in his pupil's successes. Similarly, it is just as easy to show too much disappointment when the player loses.

To be a good coach, you must not go overboard with your emotions in either direction. You should be setting about your job in such a way that you can pass judgement wisely at all times.

Correct guidance from a coach includes being able to prevent players shrinking away from their weaknesses. To me, a player who is willing to develop his game for a bright future is one who does not hide from his own weaknesses. For example, nobody misses an easy shot on purpose, and for the player to get back on the practice court and work on the easy ball as soon as he can is a positive sign.

It is extremely important that you convey to the pupil that during the match only the player can cope with the problems that crop up, but that afterwards, you will be on hand to analyse and discuss the way forward.

Player Reactions

Players react differently after defeat. Some personalities will, within moments of leaving the match, drag their coach on to the practice court – perhaps to vent their anger about a poor performance, or perhaps to rectify a particular aspect of their game which caused them disappointment and which they want to put right straightaway.

Other players are so distraught that they cannot think and will therefore avoid discussing the match or practising for several hours.

From my own coaching experience, I have learnt that everyone reacts differently. Regardless of how I feel about the situation, I always respect my players' emotions and wait for them to come to me to discuss the problems they encountered during the match.

I personally feel that, if a player is frustrated, the quicker he gets out on the practice court and lets out his frustration, the better. But I must stress that this is my personal feeling.

As a coach you must encourage the player to analyse and comment on his performance before expressing your own opinion. Otherwise, there is a strong possibility that the player will disguise his real feelings and mould his reaction to what you want or expect to hear. (You will note, when listening to players' reactions immediately following their matches, and then again perhaps a day later, how their views change, particularly where their defeats are concerned.)

It really is an art to be able to lift a player's morale and confidence when he is going through a series of bad defeats. Perhaps when a really poor streak of performances is occurring, a rest from the game may be the best answer. Again, another breed of player will do better by working still harder to get over the problem.

Defeat can naturally be very damaging to a player's outlook on the game, but the height of victory can also cloud a player's judgement – and this is where very skilful coaching will be an important factor. Use the euphoria the player is gaining from his victories to help him pursue areas of his game that are in need of development.

When a player is on a winning streak, he is generally very receptive to practising certain aspects that will develop his game. When he is not winning, he needs all the encouragement you can give him.

22
PLAYING THE BIG POINTS

If you watch the better players confronted with the important points (the so-called 'big points') you will observe that they appear to play them in the same way as any other point. Their value is not really affected.

The message here is that you should not make points so important that you cannot play them. Naturally, as your confidence develops and you gain more experience, you will discover your own way of coping with the pressure points.

Some players will take their time, possibly turning away from the server, or deliberately bouncing the ball a little longer if they are about to serve. Some players will take slow, deep breaths. Some people have suggested that you should not modify your pattern of preparation and play, in order to maintain normality.

Try and find which way of dealing with the big points best suits your physical and mental approach.

On the big points, it is especially important to know what the opposition is likely to do. Generally speaking, they will play to your weaknesses. Be ready for it. Follow your gut feelings.

I always remember Billie-Jean King saying, after being match point down against Pam Shriver in a Wimbledon quarter-final, that she knew Pam was going to go for her weaker side, her forehand, which had been deserting her for most of the match. However, she mentally geared herself up to make that one forehand, and she not only reached it, but made a superb winner from it. The psychological blow to Shriver and the boost it gave to Billie-Jean, were enough to change the entire match around, and King eventually walked off the winner.

Perhaps on that vital point Shriver

Fig 144 The mentally tough Billie-Jean King.

should have had the confidence to go for Billie-Jean's stronger backhand side. Who is to know? No wonder then, that Shriver should say that 'Billie-Jean used to mentally reach across the net and strangle you!'

There is a feeling that the player in a winning position is more likely to play it safe, trying to avoid giving the point away, and therefore, the player in the defensive position will be seeking to make him play the ball. Due to the importance of the point and the player's anxiety to win it, the 'making the play' ploy can often be rewarded.

Going for Your Shots

It is important to be aware that if you are winning by a set and 4–2, 40–15, there is a tendency for your opponent to relax because he senses that he is going to lose. He will begin to swing a little more easily at the ball.

Ironically, he is not so concerned about whether the ball goes in or out because he has almost given up mentally, but by becoming so relaxed, his game will start to flow a little more and the ball will seem to find its way into the court far more easily.

Because the pressure is not on him, he feels that he has nothing to lose and will chance his arm a little more. The result is that the match often turns around, goes into a tight final set and the pressure is reversed.

This is called 'going for your shots', a term the professionals use to explain their comeback from almost certain defeat.

But there are other styles of player. Someone like Jimmy Connors is always aggressive, whatever the situation. Players like him will always attack the ball and act like a cornered dog.

It is worth studying your opponent, just to see how he plays the big points.

Naturally, each individual develops a certain method of play at this stage, so trust your instincts, believe in yourself and do what you think is best.

Tie-Breaks

When discussing mental attitudes with my players I often suggest that in their practice sets they end up playing a tie-break. This is because the tie-break, which is here to stay as part of the modern game, is unfair. Both parties have worked hard to reach six games all and yet somebody has to win the next game to win the set. You have to accept that you have reached the point of no return, but the situation does at least apply to both players.

What is the best way of approaching the tie-break then? Do not fall into the trap of overpressing at this stage. Do not panic. Try to play each point as it comes, but be aware of all your opponent's strengths and weaknesses. You have played twelve games to reach this stage, so you should have quite a good idea of their likes and dislikes.

Of course, we all have a preference for playing in a particular style. If you are up against the precision back court player or the serve and volleyer, you will know what to expect. However, the worst type of player in a tie-break is the erratic player, the player who tends to take risks and is unpredictable.

If you do encounter such a player, just hang in there, run everything down and hope that he will eventually miss under the pressure.

With the predictable player, you know what he is going to do and what he will do well. You just have to go about the task of trying to do it even better than he does.

Because of the scoring system within the tie-break (*see* Chapter 2, page 15), a lead of 4–1 or 5–2 could quickly be whittled away. So do not be over-confident when you appear to have a comfortable lead. On the other hand, if you are the player who is 2–5 down, do not give up. You will be surprised how quickly a tie-break can turn around.

If you want to be able to play a tie-break proficiently, use your practice sets to run through four or five of them and get the feeling of the ebb and flow of the scoring system.

Winning a Set

The tie-break marks the conclusion of a set and this brings me to an area which I feel is very important. That is, the way players react to winning a set.

In particular, when a tight set has been won by a player, the latter will often relax and lose concentration. I cannot stress enough how vital it is that you should approach the next couple of games with a very positive frame of mind. A 100 per cent

Fig 145   Martina enjoying the win.

Fig 146   Agassi – the agony and the ecstasy.

application for the next couple of games can very often plant the seeds of defeat in your opponent.

However, if you relax and fail to maintain the pressure, you could find the first couple of games rapidly slipping away from you. Your opponent will then get back into the match, and before you realize it, you could be 4–2 down and in difficulties.

Once you have won a set, especially a close one, you should be ready to apply yourself and really focus on the task in hand: to win the next set as quickly as you can.

PART 5
THE MENTAL APPROACH

23
THE MATCH

To approach a match in a professional manner is of paramount importance. However, there is no set pattern in how to prepare for a match. Your own temperament will prove an extremely important factor in how you conduct yourself before, during and after a match.

There is no doubt that a player's inability to control his temperament can prove costly and damage his achievements within the game.

Despite the success that players like John McEnroe, Ilie Nastase and Hana Mandlikova have had, one can argue that if they had been in better control of their temperament they would have achieved more.

Likewise, one could argue that Bjorn Borg and Chris Evert achieved a very fine level because of their ability to keep a hold on their emotions at all times. They still are, at the time of writing, the two best exponents of concentration linked to application.

Do not be fooled. They have not become immune to pressure, rather they have learnt to enjoy the stressful situations and use them to their own benefit, knowing that their more anxious opponents may be intimidated by the situation.

Having learned to play your shots well and having gained a good tactical awareness, being in control of your temperament becomes a vital factor.

Fig 147   Bjorn Borg – famous for his nerves of steel.

Approaching the Match

Some players will prefer to keep themselves to themselves and start to concentrate on the challenge ahead perhaps two to three hours beforehand. They will blank out all conversation and hide themselves away in a corner. They might pick up a book to read, but more often than not they will just be staring at the pages.

Other players might not really like to concentrate. They will want to be in touch with everything around them and not think about the match too early – it makes them too nervous, and they feel that they are losing some of their adrenalin.

Others will be more nervous and will be looking for conversation. They will probably have their coach around, or one or two friends with whom they can chat and block out the match. They almost need to wait until being called by the referee before they begin to focus on what is going to happen.

Preparing for matches is very individualistic. You have to be aware which method best suits your own personality.

Devising a Game Plan

Usually, you will know for hours, sometimes days, beforehand, who your opponent will be. Do not waste the time available. The majority of players will be discussing with their coach or friends the strengths or weaknesses of the opposition and working out a game plan.

In your practice sessions, you can then practise and play with a method which will take advantage of the opposition's weaknesses. It is wise not to over-emphasize the tactics in practice to the extent that it affects your own style of play. Many matches are lost because the player is so concerned about what the opponent can and cannot do that he forgets his own strengths.

Before the match then, you will become aware of how your opponent plays and focus on your game plan.

If all has gone well and you have won your match, you may be waiting for your next opponent to come through. I would suggest that you and your coach go and watch his match and try and pick up some ideas on how the opponent is playing.

That is important, because even if you think you know how your opponent plays, he may have made some changes and improvements since you last saw him perform. Scouting is therefore an important part of preparing for matches.

Playing the Match

Once the match is in progress, trust in the way you play. After all, your pre-match planning and practice will hopefully pay dividends.

I suggest you start out in a match trying to impose your own strengths on your opponent. As the match develops, and if things are not quite working out as you would like, try to home in a little more on the opposition's weaknesses.

Be aware that there is always a time, when you seem to be losing, when it is beneficial to change your game plan. Exactly *when* to change is difficult to recognize. Too often, players who are struggling although their tactics are right, panic a little early and try to change their approach to the match too soon.

One match which comes to mind and reflects this was the 1988 Wimbledon semi-final when Stefan Edberg played Miloslav Mecir. For two and a half sets, Mecir was beating Edberg quite comfortably. Edberg did not change his game plan in any way and looked as if he was going to lose. Then, as Mecir missed a couple of golden opportunities, the match began to change. Mecir lost a little bit of confidence, Edberg's confidence rose and the match turned into an Edberg victory.

It was obvious that Edberg had not changed his game plan. He just carried on doing what he does best of all, serving and volleying, and kept faith in his own capabilities.

There is an art, then, in knowing when to change your own natural game and in how you should adapt to overcome the opposition. Only through experience will you understand when to apply tactical changes.

Surprisingly, it can also pay sometimes to change a winning game. You might have built a comfortable lead, but sense that your opponent is catching on to your style and game plan, and that if you continue in the same way, he will be able to reverse the trend and take control of the match.

Even though you are winning, have the courage to make changes and surprise your opponent.

You must be aware at all times not just of the need to change a losing game, but also of the changes in the mood of your opponent and of how the match is progressing.

Be Positive

The best mental approach to a match is possibly to recognize that there can only be one winner. If you have approached the match in a very professional manner, if you have practised hard, prepared sensibly and tried as hard as you could, but still lose, then you can justifiably say to yourself that you were not good enough at that particular time. However, if you keep preparing and approaching the matches in the same professional way, you will eventually achieve your goal.

Too many players are frightened of losing and therefore do not develop the courage to be positive at the right times. After all, nobody walks onto a court and deliberately plays the match to lose.

If you approach your tennis matches with the attitude that you are going to compete 100 per cent, give your all and let the match take care of itself, then you will overcome many of your fears.

How often do you see somebody playing very positive, convincing tennis, getting to a commanding position and then almost being afraid of winning?

Many players who come in sight of victory lose confidence, the rhythm of their game – and eventually, the match.

The only time you should be concerned about the win is when the umpire calls game, set and match. I remember once

seeing Zina Garrison defeat Jo Durie 6–0 6–0 at Eastbourne, and Zina admitted afterwards that she had not realized what the score was until the match was over. Her attention was focused entirely on her game and everything else was blocked out.

It is essential to play the match one point at a time. That is all you are doing, building bricks up one by one towards an eventual victory. There are no mountains to climb if you look at the match in this way.

Never try and focus on having to win an entire game or set. You do not play the game that way. Fight for each point individually. When the point is over, concentrate on the next one and so on.

In any match, the most important point is the next point – an observation that you will hear over and over again. If you think about it, you will see how true it is.

During the match, there are obviously many occasions when the value of the points becomes more important. The most important point of all, however, remains the next one, and if you are in there, fighting at all times and focusing on getting the best out of yourself, you may well find yourself winning the next point and the next.

All too often, a match is lost even though the player has set up the winning position and should be ready for the kill. Instead of focusing positively on the immediate task, he will drift into thinking about winning the next couple of games – which he expects will take him past the winning post.

It is vital not to panic and get desperate for the win, or to assume that you are home and dry before the last point has been played. There have been matches where players have led by a set, 5–0, 40–0, and still lost.

Just feel good about yourself and the position you are in at this particular stage of the match. Let it give you confidence without taking away any part of your competitive attitude. It may be easy to discuss attitude, but it is a very difficult area to put into practice.

I have found that one of the biggest assets developed by the best tennis players

The Right Attitude

Unless it is match point, another point will always come along. Develop the attitude when you play the big point and lose it, that it is just a point. Be the player who can cope with the disappointment of not making the big point. Be the one who has the ability to dismiss it. I have seen many players make an error on a crucial point but then play the next as if it were the beginning of the first set. It is an attitude and skill you have to develop over a period of time.

The player with the less pressure will be quite relaxed, going along merrily and playing quite well. But if he becomes too conscious that he has a lead and senses that he might even win the match, his reaction will be amazing.

To some extent, it is inevitable: we can all play when the pressure does not matter, but the top players have the ability to play under pressure and this is probably one of the most valuable assets you can develop.

Think positively. What is pressure? Where does it come from? Normally it comes from the expectation of winning. Where does this expectation come from? Normally it is based on the past performances of players. A player is expected to win because he has a better chance of winning. If this is pressure, give me more of it!

Remember, most pressure is self-induced.

I am quite certain that most players who have been able to perform at their best have an air of self-possession that says: 'This is the way I play, I'm going to get on with this particular style and if it's not good enough today then that's fair enough.' Overall this attitude definitely works.

If you start to go through a period during which you are not performing to the level you would like, be patient with yourself. Trust yourself. Do not start to panic.

Everybody in life goes through a rough period. Everybody has bad days at the office. Recognize that it will probably be short-lived and get out on the practice court and work as hard as ever. Believe in yourself, and you will come through the crisis. I am quite certain that no matter what style of play the top players are using, this is the philosophy they follow. They may play percentage tennis, or they may go for an all-out attack, but they have the courage to believe in their own style of play.

There will always be mini-crises during the ebb and flow of a match, but nurture the feeling of pleasure and enjoyment the battle brings.

As you begin to improve, you should be able to develop an attitude that says how much you enjoy playing, being in a position to win matches, being the person whom others are trying to beat.

Enjoy being the favourite. Think about why you are in that position (i.e. because of your superior playing record) and concentrate on playing to your potential.

Many players are on record as saying that it was tough to achieve their ranking in the game, but it was fun. They add, however, that they then found it very difficult to maintain their standard of play and keep their high ranking once they were there.

Be aware that once you have achieved a high standard, others will be out for your blood because they want the computer ranking points they will pick up by beating you, and they also crave the glory and sense of achievement. You will be a target for other players as they bid to satisfy their own ambitions.

Upon achieving a high standard, you will have to work even harder than before to make any strides forward – or even to maintain your present level.

Do not become overawed by your success and then become frightened of it all. Recognize that the game is fun.

is the ability to trust themselves and think positively at all times. They do not reveal the frustrations that might be occurring inwardly.

You must cultivate a positive attitude on the court. If you can do that – and it will take years of experience – you will be able to win.

Specialist Advice

As more and more people attempt to play tennis at a professional level, players are enlisting the help of sport psychologists and psychoanalysts. These specialists clearly have some influence, because several high class players have stated that they have benefited from the help of experts.

Sports psychologists are there to help the player think more clearly on the court and to encourage him to think in such a way that they can handle pressure. One of their main functions is to train players in anxiety reduction techniques.

Remember, however, that no matter how much psychology is used, the inevitable fact of life remains that once you venture onto the match court, you are the one who will encounter the pressure situations. Psychologists cannot hold the racquet for you and I am certain that if more players could say to themselves: "I have given it my best shot, and I could not have tried any harder – let's have fun', they would learn to come through the pressure situations on their own.

However, if you are improving your tennis, but recognize that you are unable to handle the crunch situations, then certainly seek out the help of a sports psychologist. He may well have ways and means of helping you think more clearly.

Early Development

The early breeding and education of a budding tennis player could very well be responsible for the anxieties he might encounter as his career develops.

It is the parents' responsibility to be at all times supportive. They should not put undue pressure upon the young player, by saying, for example, 'Why did you lose to that person? Why did you play so badly? How could you play such a dreadful shot?'

It will make the youngster very defensive. It will make him seek excuses, whereas a better approach could be: "Did you work your hardest today? Did you compete as well as you could have done? Did you enjoy the match?'

This will give the player the confidence to be more expressive and help him look forward to the next time he walks onto the match court.

Remember, nobody loses deliberately. Encouragement at the early stage – stressing the positive and fun elements – is a vital ingredient if players are to be able to cope with the pressures that will occur as their career develops.

It is simply not good enough to scold young players for their shortcomings in the match. Sensible discussion and debate are the most reliable ways to help them develop.

Be supportive and be progressive, which does not mean to say you should condone bad behaviour or attitude. Allow the player and encourage him to develop a positive attitude to match play.

Great damage can be caused by parents delivering the wrong message to youngsters, destroying their future development and confidence – and that can take several years to overcome.

24
PRESSURE

If you really do not enjoy the battle, then I personally believe you should not be playing the game at a competitive level. There are several players who have reached the top and decided that the game was not really for them. So, they have quit rather than put themselves through mental turmoil every time they walk onto the court.

There will always be a situation in the match when the real battle is going to come. It would be awfully boring if you won all your matches 6–0 6–0. If you talk to most of the champions, you will find that is what they miss most of all in retirement – the fun of the battle.

Do not assume that the top players have a ready-made mechanism that enables them to cope with the pressures of match play. They have had to work at it very hard.

Top players are under an enormous amount of pressure to maintain their high level of performance. They are under pressure from the media, from the opposition and also from themselves.

They have to deal with the expectations of simply winning. Some top players may win match after match and compile a winning streak of perhaps sixty-five matches. They may have even achieved five Grand Slam victories and may be going for the sixth.

Interestingly, when this winning streak is broken, it almost brings a sense of relief. It means that the players can start being constructive with their tennis again, and no longer protective of their game. During the sequence of wins, they were seeking success and a place in the record books, at the expense of experimenting to improve their game.

Fig 148 All players show emotion, sometimes even frustration, but Steffi Graf has shown the ability to come through crises.

No Pain, No Gain

This expression is one which sums up the highly professional athlete's approach to any sport.

I am not suggesting that physical toughness and extreme work rate will be the way of gaining mental toughness, but it will go a long way towards making you feel better about yourself. Then, when you walk onto a court you know you have prepared correctly for the match.

185

The Outside Agent

So far, we have discussed two types of pressure – the pressure that an opponent can bring upon you by his quality of shot, and the pressure which your nervous system brings upon yourself in a moment of crisis. But there is a third type which I would call the 'outside agent' pressure.

You can never change an opponent, nor can you change the environment, and so, before you walk onto the court, you know the circumstances that are likely to occur. You know there could be a hostile crowd and you are aware that umpires and linesmen are human and can make errors. Your opponent too might go out of his way to psyche you out.

A crowd can have an effect on your performance. Naturally, if a crowd is behind you, it will act as a stimulus and encourage you to draw the best out of yourself. However, when playing before a hostile crowd, you should rise to the challenge and use it as a means of stimulating you to play better. Show the crowd how good you are and get it on your side.

The expression 'when the going gets tough, the tough get going' applies here, and developing an attitude whereby you can deal with anything thrown at you by the crowd is vital.

Fig 149   Crowds all over the world have been enthralled by Jimmy Connors's performances during his long and dynamic career.

The majority of the better players seem able to block out all the distractions that are happening around them.

You know where you stand before you walk on court. You know the circumstances, and you simply have to get on with it. Block out the distractions, concentrate on your game and take it point by point.

Always make the best out of what is available. Manipulate the situation to suit yourself. You will not be able to change the environment you are playing in, and if you become upset by the situation, your opponent will spot it and exploit it to his advantage.

If you feel insecure, if you are almost looking for excuses, you will be vulnerable in these pressure situations.

Remember, you must prepare for any situation that may occur – mentally as well as technically and physically – before you go onto the match court. It is a philosophy that you should be able to develop over a period of time.

It will not happen overnight, but it is something the great competitors have managed to build up with their years of experience.

Knowing that you have prepared properly for the battle will give you great mental satisfaction and boost your spirits.

Some players have an advantage in obtaining certain aspects of mental toughness. Those raised on slow surfaces, clay in particular, have had to learn to rally at some length to win just one point – and then do it over and over again in the course of a match. This instinctively leads to mental toughness, because there are very few cheap points available when playing good opposition. Players brought up on faster surfaces may not learn to hang in quite as well.

There is no doubt that some players deal with pressure better than others, but if you are honest with yourself at all times you will give yourself every opportunity of trusting yourself at important stages of match play.

Over the years, many players of the

Fig 150 Throughout his career, McEnroe has gone through tremendous emotional pressure to succeed.

highest standing have been labelled losers or chokers. Yet they stuck to their task, battled hard, believed in themselves at all times and came through to become fine champions. Two all-time greats, Margaret Court and Ivan Lendl were dubbed losers. They both worked exceedingly hard at achieving their goals and many players would be envious of their track records.

Mental toughness can only come from standing up and being counted in pressure situations. Do not shirk them. Look forward to them and enjoy the battles.

Have the courage to look within yourself objectively and discuss with your coach after the matches how you felt during moments of crisis. This will help you understand and identify the problems that might occur in the future, and how to combat them.

25

DEALING WITH BAD LINE CALLS

In any match, you could run into a series of bad line calls, some of which might be absolutely crucial.

Of course it is frustrating to see that a point you have laboured for has been lost through an injustice. The tragedy is that mistakes can occur at very important stages in a match, but so can the mistakes that you yourself make. These might amount to thirty or forty, as opposed to the two or three at most that the umpire or linesmen have made.

So be aware that, in the absence of some modern technological way of calling the lines, a human error factor has to play a part in any match.

There is absolutely no point at all in arguing a line call decision – it will not be changed. A line call, if not immediately over-ruled by the umpire will not be altered. You are merely wasting energy that would be better spent preparing yourself for the next point. The previous point has been lost and there is nothing you can do about it. Forget it, swallow your anger and channel your frustrations into thinking positively about the next point.

Of course, if a point of law is in dispute

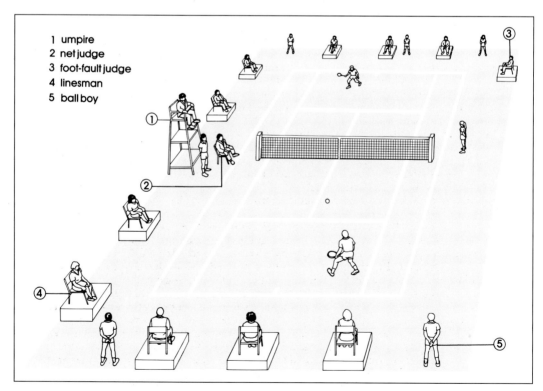

1 umpire
2 net judge
3 foot-fault judge
4 linesman
5 ball boy

Fig 151   Positions of umpire, linesmen and ball boys.

The View from the Umpire's Chair

Few tournament players go through their career without suffering from what they believe to be incompetent officiating, or without believing that an umpire or linesman has been against them in a particular match. Understanding the way these officials operate may help you in your own game, especially in tense moments when you think a particular linesman is 'out to get you'.

Sultan Ganji is one of Britain's top referees. He has umpired at all tournament levels, including the US Open and Wimbledon, where one of his matches was the semi-final between Stefan Edberg and Miloslav Mecir. Sultan also overlooks most of the tournaments in Africa, working for the International Tennis Federation (ITF). His experience might be of help:

Most umpires are amateurs who have joined an Umpires Association because they have either played tennis themselves or just enjoy the game. They do the job voluntarily and pay their own expenses at tournaments. The fact that most umpires take holidays or unpaid leave from their usual work to officiate at tournaments is not always realized by the players. However, some professional umpires are now being employed to work full-time on the professional circuit.

The standard of the tournament really dictates the standard of umpires who will work there. At county or regional level, you will find the 'beginner' umpires who are just learning the trade. The higher grade umpires are present at Satellite and Challenger tournaments. Two or three top grade umpires will officiate the most awkward matches, between players who have been known to be troublesome. There will also be a few second grade umpires, as well as those who have come through the junior ranks and are there for the experience.

If the umpire wears an official ITF badge then he is an experienced and respected official, so a minimal number of problems are to be expected on court. Unfortunately, and almost inevitably, there are players on the tour who are guilty of gamesmanship and poor behaviour. It is imperative for the umpire to deal firmly, but politely, with the slightest sign of petulance, which generally will gain him the player's respect.

Obviously, the umpire has ways of controlling the match if it does start to get out of hand. There is a penalty system whereby a player can be warned for ball and racquet abuse, as well as for visible or audible obscenity. These rules are called 'code violations' and are really public warnings. They help keep a temperamental player under control.

Every tournament has a referee whose responsibility starts even before the tournament begins. He must deal with entry lists – making the draw and the order of play for each day. It is his job to interpret the rules of tennis throughout the entire competition. Players usually know the referee quite well because they see that person frequently and can comunicate freely with him.

The referee is the final authority on the rules. He is paid to do that job because it is a full week's work, starting before the first ball is struck right through to the very end. He also has to work with the tournament committee in setting up the competition.

Some players believe that one official might be on an ego trip and intent on showing that he, and not the player, is in control of the match. I would be wrong to say that does not occur, but if you take the British Tennis Umpires Association (BTUA), you will see that it contains nearly 450 amateurs. It is inevitable that in such a large group there should be a few who are different from the rest. Each umpire has his own character and style of officiating, some good, and some bad.

From my personal point of view, a top grade umpire is one who lets the match flow smoothly, without exerting his authority on the match – except under extreme circumstances. If a player believes that he is suffering from an inefficient official, my advice to him is to realize that all officials have gone through a training and grading process from C2 to A1.

The manager of umpires and the referee between them try and select the right type of umpire for the player. Occasionally mistakes are made because the decision relies on judging what is likely to be an easy or difficult match. Remember, the umpire is trying his best.

If a player sincerely feels he is getting a raw deal from the umpire, I would suggest he ask for the referee. When I referee, I will then sit by the side of the court for two or three games. It helps the player to calm down, because he realizes I am competent, and if I think the match is going badly I will have the umpire or offending linesman replaced. All the officials are aware that I am there because there has been a complaint and it has an effect. Inevitably, my presence leads to the umpire and linesmen concentrating harder. The referee, then, is there to ensure the smooth running of a match and to achieve a fair result for both players.

We do not take sides. Our satisfaction is to see matches go through smoothly.

Fig 152   Ilie Nastase – a genius without doubt, but how much more would he have achieved with better control over his temperament?

come through any crisis created by a bad line call.

If tennis players looked back on their whole career and studied all the matches they have played, not more than half a dozen could say that an umpire or linesman cost them the match.

If you are to pursue tennis at the highest level, you cannot allow yourself to become preoccupied with poor decisions, hostile crowds, or mis-hits that your opponent might make.

Once you get used to blaming outside agents for any of your own failings, your mental system will play upon your inability to cope with such situations. Ninety-five per cent of the time, when players start to look for excuses they are covering up their own inadequacies in coping with the pressure.

There is no doubt that if you are good enough, your tennis will win the day. If you are not able to deal with the battle and frustrations of match play, then certain areas of your game are probably not good enough. The answer then, is to get back to the drawing board and the practice court and work even harder to rectify the problem.

I can remember listening to Rod Laver being interviewed after a defeat he suffered at the important stage of a major championship. He offered no excuses and quite simply admitted that on that particular day the other player had been too good for him and that he was going to return to the practice court and make sure that, when they met again, he would be able to take his revenge. This was the same Rod Laver who took time off to improve his serve when he was already number one in the world!

then – and only then – can the tournament referee intervene and make a ruling. He cannot and will not become involved in line call disputes. Do not waste your energy on arguing otherwise. It is counter-productive.

Similarly, there is no sense in losing your temper in matches. If you are not in control of your emotions, then you are not in control of the match. Your opponent will simply gain confidence and draw strength from your weakness.

Without doubt, there are some players whom it suits to blame the umpire or the linesman, or any other distraction. Again, those who are mentally tougher will best

If you are to become a tough match player, you have to recognize your own failings and work hard to eradicate your weaknesses.

PART 6
DOUBLES

26
PLAYING DOUBLES

Generally speaking, all aspiring tennis players – when first starting out – begin by playing singles. Then as time goes by, unless they intend to pursue the game seriously, the majority become competent club players and will almost inevitably play more doubles than singles. It is a simple fact of life that ninety per cent of club tennis is built around the social game of doubles and without doubt, there is a difference between the two games.

When playing singles, you can successfully build your style of game from the baseline, and even as you develop an all-court game, the necessity to be competent from the baseline will still be of paramount importance. However, the game of doubles will require you to become an efficient net player, because the general game plan revolves around building a successful net attack.

As discussed in Chapters 4 and 5, to be a successful net player will require not only a high quality approach, together with the ability to play sound volleys and overheads, but also the knowledge of where your opponent will attempt to pass or lob you.

In doubles, though, by virtue of having two players at each end – which naturally means that two people are able to cover the court – the net attack is a great deal easier to achieve. It is inevitable that when the net position is achieved, whether the net player or the baseliner wins the point, the rallies will usually be much shorter.

Therefore, to be a successful doubles player, you will have to develop a good volley, a good smash and also a very reliable serve and volley game.

Unlike singles, where the surface will have a large influence on the style of play, the doubles game and the tactics that are employed will be the same on all surfaces, even the slowest clay. However, I would add that it is easier to play a rearguard baseline action on a slower surface than on a faster surface and therefore, occasionally, a successful backcourt doubles team can be effective on the slow clay courts.

If you really do wish to develop a successful doubles game, you will have to be efficient and competent with your repertoire of shots at the net. At tournament level, the most successful team, be it men or women, will be the one that is most effective from the net. However, at club level, women's teams can be successful by playing from the baseline. But to get some fun out of doubles, it is worth having the confidence to develop a net game as well.

The Serve in Doubles

Generally speaking, very few servers in doubles will remain on the baseline after their serve. It can be used as a tactic but I would recommend a serve-and-volley ploy most of the time.

As the doubles court is wider than a singles court and since four people are participating in the game, the value of angles tends to be far more important in doubles than in singles. (This is not to suggest that knowing the angles does not form an important part of singles – it definitely does – but many more angle shots will be used in doubles.)

If you really do wish to become an effective doubles player, it will pay to develop quick reactions, because as the rallies tend to be shorter and quicker, you can often find yourself in situations where

Fig 153   Martina has made good use of her serve throughout her illustrious career.

all four players are at the net. Naturally, this means that you have less time to prepare and play the ball and it will therefore be worth practising some exercises, such as volleying in pairs (*see* Part 3).

Because your partner's standard position when you are serving is at the net, the angles are already created for the return of serve. Similarly, when you are coming in behind your serve, you will have less court to cover because your partner is at the net and is responsible for certain returns.

The role of the net player partnering the server is to protect his tramline, to be able to cover the lob – he will therefore need to have an excellent smash – and at the same time to recognize a poor return which can be intercepted for a potential kill volley.

When watching a high standard doubles match, note that the players will very rarely serve full out with flat serves. They will sometimes use it as a tactical ploy, but generally speaking they will use variations of spin – in particular the kick serve which gives them more time to get to the net and so achieve an attacking position alongside their partner.

Where should you stand when your partner is serving? Clearly, this is a matter for personal preference, but I would recommend standing approximately 1.8–2.4m (6–8ft) from the net and about 90cm–1.8m (3–6ft) in from the inner tramline. This will give you the opportunity to cover the return down your tramline, or the lob, and at the same time give you the chance to intercept a poor return.

Having said that, there are no hard and fast rules. You need to make whatever preparations are necessary to cover the opposition's favourite shots.

As you develop your doubles game, you will improve by experience your understanding of where to stand.

The Return of Serve in Doubles

When you return serve in doubles, the angles are already created for you – as one of the opposition will almost always be based at the net. To be successful at returning serve, experiment with the following methods.

Normally, you should be seeking to return the ball low over the net, away from the opposition's net player. You can attempt that by using heavy topspin – which will dip the ball low over the net – or the slow dink – which is more difficult to execute and therefore requires a delicate touch. Either way, you are hoping that this type of return will cause the incoming server to either half-volley or play a difficult low volley – which will then put the opposition in a defensive situation.

Another type of return could be to lob the net player. Essentially, you will not expect a winner from this shot, but you will be hoping that you and your partner, if the lob is effective, will then be able to take over the aggressive net position.

Another return is to try and play down the tramline of the player at the net. Since the net player is already in position to cover that return, it has to be a high quality shot. However, there are certain times when it can be beneficial. One obvious time is to use it as a surprise return, and another is when the net player is intercepting frequently and you seek out the tramline to frustrate that particular ploy (*see* Fig 154) .

Of course, you can also try to hit the ball straight to the middle of the opposition's court (*see* Fig 155).

When you are returning serve, your partner will be standing in a position which threatens a net attack – i.e. within 60 or 90cm (2 or 3ft) of the inside of the service line and approximately half way between the tramline and the centre service line.

You will notice that he will not be as close to the net as the server's partner. This is because he now has the ability to recognize the type of return you have hit which allows him to do one of two things:

1.   If you have hit a high quality return he should be looking for the opportunity to advance forward, threaten the opposition and look for a kill position himself.

2. If you have hit a poor return, his position enables him to scamper back to the baseline and set up a defensive formation so that you may both, as a team, get back into the rally.

If you are struggling to make an impression on the opposition's serve and are losing those games easily, try this as a tactic. Suggest that your partner comes back to the baseline with you. This can change the angles of the net player's volleys and throw him off his guard.

Also, if your opponents are sending down very aggressive serves and you are unable to make threatening returns, stand

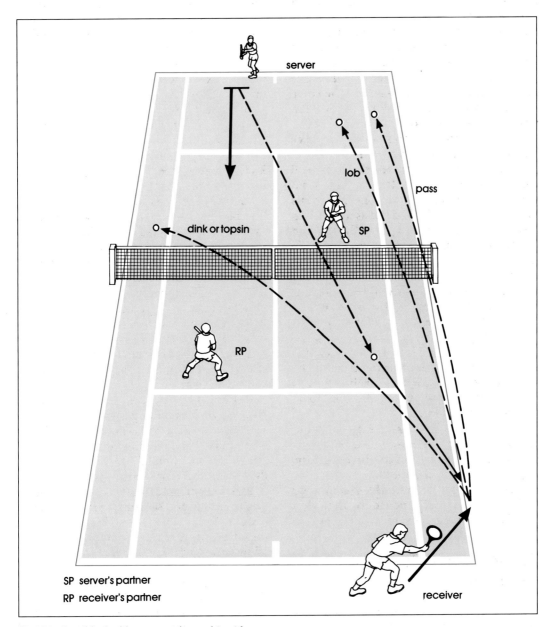

Fig 154 Possible doubles return of serve hit wide.

Fig 155 Possible doubles return of serve hit down the middle.

back, lob the serve and create defensive rallies. This can have a damaging effect on opponents whose game plan will now have to change. Be patient when using this ploy, as it may take a while before a series of hoisted, high lobs start to affect the opposition's confidence. You will find that it can earn you a break of serve on some occasions.

The Australian Formation

A good plan for servers struggling against someone who is returning very well is the Australian Formation. In playing this, you encourage your partner to stand much closer to the net, but on your side of the centre service line. This will force the returner of serve, who has been using the cross-court angle so effectively, to hit down the line or possibly try a very quick lob.

Again, you will be surprised how this can throw the opposition off their track. After perhaps two or three points played that way, go back to an orthodox position.

Try these ideas. They can only broaden your horizons, and at the same time cause problems to the opposition. Do not be afraid of experimenting.

The Importance of the First Volley

Successful doubles players really do work hard on their volley, but they especially need to be very able on the first volley. (The first volley is the one that is played after the serve.) This has to be developed into a confident and reliable shot.

As discussed earlier, the emphasis when serving is not necessarily on pace or weight of shot, it is on spin, linked to a high percentage of first serves. This, in turn, will set you up in a confident and sound position to play an effective first volley.

In practice sets, try to play without looking for aces on the first serve. Deliberately spin the first serve into play in a manner that will encourage the opposition to make their return so that you will have to make a volley behind your serve. It will surprise you how much your confidence will build up as you develop your serve-and-volley game.

Some Variations

You should now have a basic understanding of how the doubles game is played. I shall now give you some tips, ideas and variations on which to work.

One of the features of good doubles play is the value of interception. This really is an art in itself, but with some smart practice and application you will be able to improve your game in this vital area quite considerably. Without doubt, to play doubles at the highest level, the ability to intercept is essential. It breaks up the pattern of play and causes the opposition some uncertainty. They will become more and more aware of the likelihood of the interceptor moving. This could cause the opposition to panic and offer easy balls for the interceptor to kill.

One major area when learning to intercept is that you must not be afraid of being passed. It is inevitable that you will be. Even the finest doubles players in the world can make the wrong moves. You must understand that the constant threat of an interceptor can be just as damaging as the shots themselves.

Naturally, you will need to have quick reactions in order to intercept. However, be aware that another key is the ability to use your vision – to anticipate what the opposition will be doing. You should also be able to recognize that your partner has also created pressure by the quality of his serve or return, which will give you the opportunity to set up an interception (*see* Figs 156 and 157).

This is probably one of the most exciting aspects of developing your doubles game, and when watching a high level doubles match, it is the thrill of watching the speed and reaction time of the net players that excites the spectators.

If you really want to progress and improve your doubles, do not be frightened of learning to intercept – it will pay handsome dividends in the end.

The Effect of Different Surfaces

I suggested earlier that the variations of surface will have little effect on the basic tactics used by doubles teams. However, there can be some adaptations to faster or slower surfaces.

When you are serving on a quicker court, or a surface that causes a low bounce, try and slice the ball more. On the slower surfaces, or those that cause a high bounce, use the kick or topspin serve.

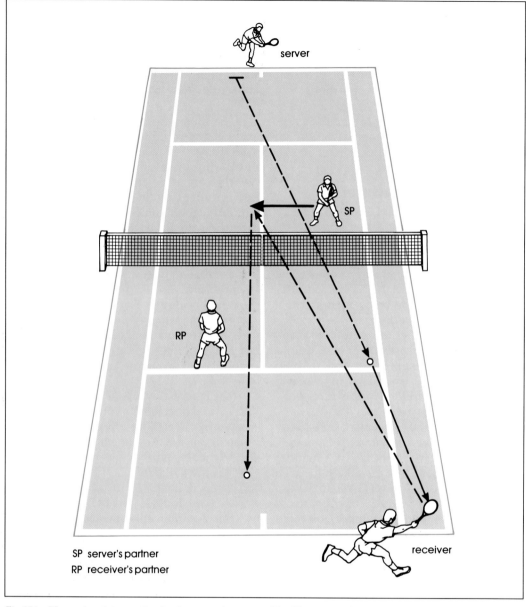

Fig 156   Elementary interception by the server's partner. The illustration shows
how a poor service return down the middle of the court can be intercepted by
the server's partner and played into the gap between the receiver and the
receiver's partner.

The returner of serve will adapt his game
too. For example, on the faster surfaces, the
returner should attempt to threaten the
server by taking the ball much earlier. This
is accomplished by taking less of a backswing and using a blocking action to take
the pace off the ball. On the slower surfaces, where there is more time, the returner could stand further back to give himself
more room to allow him to use a fuller
swing and thus generate more pace or
topspin.

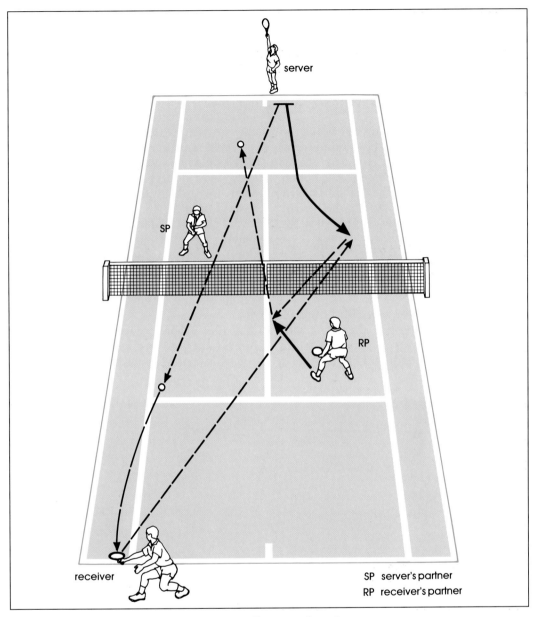

Fig 157 Interception by the receiver's partner. The illustration shows how a
good return of serve by the receiver has created a gap in the middle of the court
and the receiver's partner can intercept the server's first volley for a winner.

Using Signals

Over the years, some doubles teams have
tried working with the signals theory. The
most successful and effective teams to use
this tactic in recent times have been Bob

Hewitt and Frew McMillan and Patty Fen-
dick and Jill Hetherington.

Essentially, the use of signals operates
by means of a very simple code. The net
player clenching his fist, opening his hand
or pointing his finger will indicate to the

199

server whether he will or will not move once the returner has struck the ball. Naturally, you would have to play with your partner over a period of time to develop the team work required for this particular tactic. It would also be beneficial to go onto the practice court first to experiment with the idea.

It is important, once you have made the communication, that you both honour the signal that has been made. If the net player indicates that he will intercept, the server should then be protecting the side of the court to which he would not normally run.

It does require definite planning for the tactic to be successful.

Team Work

An important asset for successful doubles teams is good comradeship. Practising with your partner helps you to merge smoothly as a team and understand each other's strengths and weaknesses. Without doubt, to be a successful team over a long period of time, communication is a vital factor – just look at the Navratilova–Shriver partnership.

When watching good doubles teams, you will notice that they are normally always talking to each other on the court, whether they are wining or losing the match.

I have seen some combinations who, as singles players, were inadequate, but who – by good understanding and combining their own strengths and weaknesses – made a fine duo. Conversely, it does not always follow that if you are a good singles player, you will automatically be a good doubles player.

One obvious reason is that a fine singles player needs a tunnel-vision approach. When playing singles, you can cope with your own mistakes, but at doubles, you may find it hard to accept your partner's errors, and therefore you might sometimes react very unfavourably in these situations.

Fig 158   Navratilova and Shriver – a devastating combination who have amassed numerous Grand Slam titles.

One of the arts of playing successfully at doubles is being able to make your partner feel comfortable at all times, no matter how torrid a time he may be going through.

Because of the very nature of the doubles game, you will very rarely find rallies going beyond ten strokes. Doubles can therefore attract a certain type of player who may struggle to be a success at singles because of an inability to sustain rallies. However, their mentality and style of play can often combine successfully in a doubles format at the highest level.

One player who has been ranked consistently in the top ten at doubles and has won several Grand Slam events is Elizabeth Smylie from Australia, even though, during the same period, her singles ranking once dropped as low as 170.

One of the reasons behind doubles success as opposed to singles struggle is the psychological approach.

In doubles, players can share responsibility with their partner and draw strength from the way they think and react to certain situations, and likewise, they can assist their partner through a crisis too. But when they are playing singles, they are simply not strong enough mentally to cope with the loneliness of the singles game.

Benefits to the Singles Player

There are two aspects of doubles which I think can be beneficial to singles players:

1. If you are primarily a baseliner, but would like to develop some confidence in your net attack, playing some doubles may help. The very nature of the game will encourage you to volley more. Many players who have had successful singles careers based around their solid back court game have then developed confidence to volley more by playing doubles. Chris Evert undoubtedly improved her volleying, and Ivan Lendl has made an effort to play doubles. In both cases I am sure the benefit has been shown in their improved net play.

2. Playing doubles can help if you are going through a bad spell and not winning matches. You can stop the rot by playing and winning some doubles matches. This will restore your confidence and will be reflected in your performance on the singles court.

Advice for Women Players

At international level, there is no difference between the way in which the top women and the top men develop their style of play. It is based around a sensible net attack.

However, at club level, the difference becomes quite apparent. Women players are in many cases far more comfortable playing from the back of the court, and there is without doubt a general fear of the net position.

Be confident! I can assure you that by developing the confidence to go to the net and by learning to volley better you will improve your doubles performance by leaps and bounds.

Seek out a good coach either on an individual or a group basis. With some patience and sensible tuition you will learn to play the volley in a far more confident manner, which in turn will improve your doubles performance.

Mixed Doubles

Mixed doubles are played sociably more than any other form of tennis and should, as such, remain sociable. Mixed doubles at club level are supposed to be fun.

However, if you look at the international scene, mixed doubles can be taken very seriously. After all, if you enter a Grand Slam event it can be financially rewarding and very satisfying to get your name engraved on the trophy.

If you play mixed doubles at that level, you must be aware, when the stakes are high, that the male opposition may play very aggresively towards you. Because of

Fig 159   Jo Durie and Jeremy Bates winning the Mixed Doubles at Wimbledon in 1987.

the strength of the man's serve, he is rarely broken and the emphasis tends to be on breaking your serve.

If you are going to play successful mixed doubles, you must develop a reliable serve-and-volley game. This will enable you to play competently enough to hold your own. If you are able to win your serve (with some assistance from your partner) you will develop into an able mixed doubles player.

When you are returning serve in mixed doubles, be very positive and attack. Do not try and play too defensively because the male player will pick up and intercept your return. If you seek to be aggressive and play winners you can be far more threatening and frustrate the male opposition.

Generally speaking, successful male players at mixed doubles really do intimidate the female players. So, beat them at their own game, look to intercept and impose yourself. Be positive, and play in a positive manner.

PART 7
COURT SURFACES

27
COURT SURFACES – THEIR INFLUENCE

Since 1968, when tennis became a professional sport and was termed 'Open', the popularity of the various court surfaces has ebbed and flowed.

When Rod Laver was winning his Grand Slams, three of the venues used grass courts and the other used clay. It can be argued that it is far more difficult to win the Grand Slam under present day conditions because it is played on four different surfaces. The French Open uses clay, the US Open uses a cement hardcourt, the Australian Open uses Rebound Ace (which looks similar to the US Open surface but is rubberized and softer) and Wimbledon is now the only venue which uses grass.

The reason for the change is, quite simply, that to produce high quality grass courts is a particularly difficult job, and with the tennis industry booming as it has done, the requirement of the top class players is for top class courts. The other major factor is that climate will dictate the quality of grass courts in a particular country and also what surfaces can be used all year round.

In North America, cement is the most popular surface, although in Florida they have green clay courts too. In Europe and South America, a red – or more precisely a burnt orange – clay court is preferred. In Australia, grass is probably still the most popular surface, but now that the Australian Open is using Rebound Ace, several of the big clubs are changing to that surface also. In the UK, natural grass is now also a dying surface and is being replaced by synthetic grass which is extremely popular with club members but, in my opinion, is not conducive to producing good tennis players.

With the increased worldwide interest in tennis, indoor centres are becoming very popular. In many of these, a synthetic carpet is used as well as a surface called Supreme – a synthetic rubberized material known as polymeric.

Another popular surface in the UK is one termed as 'all-weather'. It is of a tarmac base construction upon which paint is sprayed.

The range of surfaces now used means that players face a greater challenge if they are to succeed on the world tour, as they must be able to adapt readily to the variations of surface. They must be far more versatile than the players of the past.

The clay court game is totally different to the grass court game, and even apparently similar hardcourt or carpet surfaces can vary in speed according to how they are laid. Good players must therefore always be ready and able to adapt.

Some surfaces will naturally favour and encourage you to serve and volley while others will encourage you to stay back around the baseline.

Grass

When discussing grass court play, I believe, with some rare exceptions that the men players will have to play a serve and volley game, more so than in the women's game, where success can also be achieved by being a reliable baseliner.

Grass is a fast surface. The ball tends to skid off the turf and if sidespin or slice is put on the ball, it will keep very low. Grass therefore suits a more attacking style of play and that is why the majority of players will serve and volley.

Traditionally, the men's champion at Wimbledon has been a serve and volleyer, but there have been exceptions – most notably, Bjorn Borg. However, there have been very strong arguments put forward that Borg was able to dominate on grass because of the changes of surface for the major events. This meant that many more players had to develop an all-court style of play, which in turn implied that far fewer out-and-out serve-and-volley style players would be effective on grass courts. Could Borg have been so effective on grass thirty years earlier, when there were so many good Australian and American natural serve and volleyers whom he would have had to overcome?

Quite frankly, you do not need to have a particularly well-rounded game to be a successful grass court player. Several players have achieved success at Wimbledon purely on the strength and quality of their serve backed up by a competent volley.

Because women are unable to generate as much pace as the men, there has been a balance of styles which have been successful over the years. Margaret Court, Billie-Jean King and Martina Navratilova have been successful with a natural serve-and-volley style, while baseline players such as Maureen Connolly, Chris Evert and Steffi Graf have also been champions.

Of all the surfaces, with the exception of an indoor wooden surface, grass will probably be the fastest. As the surface is so quick it is very difficult to sustain long rallies. It is therefore advantageous to use a serve-and-volley or net game, whereas all the other surfaces are probably more conducive to the groundstroke style of player.

Clay

While grass courts seem to be fading in popularity, clay which is common in Europe and South America is gaining ground.

A clay surface, despite its name, is not clay-based. It is actually a thoroughly ground-down brick, which when compacted produces an excellent playing surface.

It is forgiving on the legs, but requires a high degree of maintenance. It needs to be well-watered and dragged with a brush to produce an even playing surface.

At all the championship events that use clay, there is a necessity after each match for the court to be treated by the ground staff, so it can be returned to a good playing condition.

As the player moves to the ball and makes his last couple of strides, he is able to actually slide into the shot, but these slide marks will marginally cut up the playing surface. The damage done to the surface during the match can lead to some frustrating bad bounces. Bearing in mind, though, the severe treatment the court will receive from the players' footwork, the problem is negligible.

At the time of writing, there appears to be a large group of players, brought up on clay courts, who are very successful (*see* Fig 00). This has led to a growing feeling within the coaching fraternity that the need to play on clay at the early stages of learning the game is essential.

To play successfully on a clay court, considerable patience is required because the surface tends to play slowly, i.e. the ball moves slowly off the surface. It allows players the opportunity to run down and retrieve the ball, whereas on a grass court the ball moves quickly off the court, making retrieving more difficult. If the ball is bouncing off the surface slowly, it gives players more time to recover and the rallies will usually be extended – sometimes to thirty, forty or fifty shots – and players have to learn patience to play successfully.

Traditionally, the majority of clay court players will play from the back of the court because there is time to retrieve the ball, whereas attacking from the net is a little more difficult. However, one of the features of playing on a clay court is that it encourages players to develop more variety and imagination within their game and the tactics they employ.

Essentially, what you need to perform well on a clay court is consistency linked to patience, and a variety of accurate topspin and slice groundstrokes as well as tactical awareness.

It is imperative if you wish to play effectively on a clay court that you develop a running pattern which enables you to slide into your shots when you are playing the ball on the run. This way, the player can meet the ball, play the shot and recover almost simultaneously.

There is no doubt that becoming a successful clay court player really will broaden your horizons in terms of tactics. Of all the surfaces that you may use, it is probably the one on which the drop shot is most effective.

If you do attack, be cautious. To do so effectively will require the ability to select the right ball on which to approach the net, because the surface is slow enough for your opponent to chase the ball down. He will then have sufficient time to pick his passing shot or lob.

It is worth mentioning how several great players in the past have been successful in winning Wimbledon and the US and Australian Opens, but have found it very difficult to win the French Open. They have struggled to adapt their style. In recent times, some obvious players are Jimmy Connors and John McEnroe. Other players such as Bjorn Borg have had such a strong mental discipline that they could survive and play point after point, match after match, with an incredible degree of patience.

In the history of the French Championships, there have only been seven American champions. The reason often given is that the majority of men from the States are very able on cement courts where the ball bounces much faster, generally over waist-height, and their technique is geared to taking the ball early. Due to the greater length of time the clay court player will have to strike the ball, topspin is favoured much more on this surface than any other.

Very few American players use excessive topspin, while it is used so successfully by the South Americans and Europeans.

One drawback of clay courts – and indeed grass courts – is that they both need a high level of grooming if they are to be maintained in a proper manner. This implies a large number of ground staff and reflects why, in the UK at least, there are very few clubs that can provide excellent grass or clay courts. The clubs simply cannot afford the costs involved.

Cement

This is one of the most used surfaces, particularly in the US. It is generally termed a 'perfect surface', because it is usually guaranteed to provide the perfect bounce. On grass courts, variations in the soil and weather conditions will always affect the bounce. On clay courts, uneven areas and perhaps some sand from a slide will sometimes cause odd bounces.

Cement courts encourage and support players who require a perfect bounce. They also tend to produce a certain type of player: when you have been brought up on a cement court and are guaranteed a reliable bounce, you can anticipate exactly where the ball will land and there will be little need for improvisation.

There is no doubt that players who are brought up on grass and clay have to learn to improvise because there is a likelihood of changing bounces. They have to be on their guard and ready to change their shot.

Typical cement-surface players include Chris Evert, Jimmy Connors, Andre Agassi and Michael Chang. Obviously, they each have individualistic traits within their own technique. However, they are a perfect reflection of the modern American player.

The only way in which cement courts can vary is in the speed of the bounce, and this is dependent on the way the final coating of paint is applied. But overall, a cement court surface will always be true and predictable.

Referring again to Chris Evert and Jimmy Connors, you will note how so many

American players since the early to mid-seventies have copied them and developed the two-fisted backhand linked to a very simplistic style of forehand takeback.

This particular method of play is encouraged because there is no fear of receiving a poor bounce. Perhaps in recent times this has become one of the drawbacks to the Americans producing more world-class champions? I am quite sure that if the American coaches encouraged a little more variety in style in their up-and-coming youngsters it would be a catalyst in helping the Americans to produce their next World Number One.

One disadvantage of cement is that because it is such a hard and unforgiving surface, it can be damaging to the knees and ankle joints. In recent times many players have also suffered from shin splints as a result of playing too much on cement.

Rebound Ace

Rebound Ace, at this moment in time, is a surface used for tournament play only in Australia. It is similar in many ways to cement but it has a rubber content which makes it a little more comfortable to play on. It is more forgiving on the players' legs.

Like cement, it produces the perfect bounce, and perhaps as a result we shall see fewer Australians with a traditional serve-and-volley style – the trademark of Australia's grass courts.

Synthetic Grass

Before beginning to discuss indoor surfaces, I think it is worth mentioning that in the UK clubs are now encouraged to use synthetic grass. This is a synthetic carpet with a sand base. The sand is spread loosely between the synthetic fibres and allowed to bed down.

I am personally very disappointed about the introduction of this surface purely for selfish reasons, because I am desperately interested in British players improving at an international level. To date, there has not been a top class international event that has used this surface.

Top class players are ill at ease moving on the surface, often feeling uncomfortable when moving quickly to a ball, and lacking confidence that they will be in control of their physical recovery for the next shot.

However, I can totally understand the merits of the surface for club play. With the dreadful British climate, the surface can be used all year round and it is heartening to see club members playing throughout the winter months. Another plus factor is that after a deluge of rain, the courts are playable again very quickly, although the balls may get fairly heavy.

Unfortunately, while it may make club members happy, it is not conducive to producing world-class tennis players. It is interesting to note that Australia – which was one of the first countries to lay the surface – is now replacing it with Rebound Ace.

Indoor Surfaces

Tennis is now generating so much interest worldwide that in the last fifteen years or so there has been a boom in the opening of indoor venues.

Any indoor tennis courts fifteen or twenty years ago would usually have been constructed of a wood-based surface. Now there are just a handful of these in existence. Quite simply, the surface is so quick that it is very difficult for club members of an elementary level to gain any fun or benefit from the game. In fact, if the men's game at international level was played on wood, I believe the attendance would decline because the game would be so boring. It would consist merely of a series of service games held.

The most fequently used indoor surfaces are carpets, the most common type being called 'Supreme'. It is very resilient, it can be rolled up and although heavy, stored easily. Supreme is extremely popular at tournament level and is used at more than

300 events in over forty countries. The All England Club at Wimbledon has also installed it in their new indoor centre.

The under-surface upon which the carpet or Supreme is laid will determine the speed of the ball off the surface and the height of the bounce. It is often laid on wood or cement.

Most indoor surfaces are medium-paced, which encourages a variety of styles: serve and volley can be as effective as baseline play. Spectators are then able to watch good competitive matches at indoor venues.

Adjusting to Surfaces

Changing surfaces should not be taken lightly, because of the variation in speed and bounce. Efforts should be made to find a practice court upon which you can adjust your game before going to a tournament.

There is considerable dissension at the closeness between the French Open and Wimbledon, because many players feel they have too little time to adjust their game from clay to grass. Some top players therefore sacrifice Paris in order to perfect their grass court game for Wimbledon, or alternatively they avoid tournaments between the French Open and Wimbledon so that they can practise endlessly without the additional pressure of computer points.

Benefits of a Changing World

To some extent it is important to look at tennis as an industry and see how the boom in professional tennis in the last fifteen years or so have influenced the game.

Traditions have changed or are changing, and that plays an important part in the way club players are reared and encouraged to play. For example, if beginners were to play indoors on a wooden court, they would probably feel the surface was too quick. They would be unable to deal with the fast bounce and would feel out of their depth. As a result, they might well turn to other sports for recreation.

So, the way the surfaces have changed has made the game more approachable to beginners and club players and that is beneficial to the game as a whole.

Tennis is really moving into the twenty-first century, and not only with the advancement in court surfaces. Investigate the incredible choice of tennis shoes now on the market. Shoes are now designed to take into account the surface on which they will be used. They enable you to move successfully and effectively on different surfaces (*see* Chapter 3, page 26).

It is therefore worth seeking out professional advice when you are looking to buy your next pair of shoes. Perhaps it could give you that extra edge over the opposition.

PART 8
INJURY

28
COMMON PROBLEMS

Poor technique can be responsible for causing injuries, in particular to the back, neck, shoulder, elbow and wrist, and advanced players are as susceptible to injury as beginners.

One common problem is tendinitis. This can be caused by incorrect gripping and poor control of the racquet when playing your strokes. It can also result from using too light or too heavy a racquet, or too big or too small a grip.

Be terribly careful when purchasing a racquet from a sports shop. My advice to anyone who is taking up the game is that before they buy their equipment, they should seek out a professional at his own shop or club. He will be aware of which type and weight will suit your own style and will give you objective advice.

Seek out the professional too, for coaching at the early stages, as he will encourage you to learn a sound method. This is very important because many players later suffer from the effects of poor technique.

Poor serving and smashing technique can lead to serious back problems. Be wise; it is definitely worth putting in the extra effort to learn a correct stroke even if it does not feel natural at first.

Make sure you are wearing the appropriate shoes for the surface. If the shoes are incorrect, you can have too little grip or too much, leading to sprained ankles or Achilles' heel trouble. Some players today wear shoes with the higher back to protect their Achilles' heel.

You can lose months of play because of injury so take precautions very seriously. Lessons can save you an enormous amount of trouble and pain in later years as well as benefiting your game.

Advice from an Expert

Donna Pallulat is a certified athletic trainer who worked for the Women's International Tennis Association from 1981 until 1989. One of the leading figures in her field, with Bachelor and Master degrees from San Diego State University, she has tended to the needs of the world's top players at various tournaments around the world and also worked as the Australian Federation Cup team's trainer. She explains briefly what causes the most common injuries and how they can be prevented and treated:

There is no way of predicting when or what injuries may occur to those who are participating at an elite level, but people who are not in good condition and have poor mechanics are going to have more injuries.

You can look at the weekend player who picks up his racquet and does not stretch, who uses a racquet with old strings and plays with dead balls and you can pick out the injuries that they are likely to sustain.

A player must have good equipment, properly maintained, and that equipment must be suited to him. The weight of the racquet and the string tension must match his technique.

If you have poor technique, then you do not play with a highly-strung racquet because this will give vibrations up the arm. It can also lead to muscle strain, ligament irritation, joint irritation and tendinitis.

The most common injuries are in the shoulder – rotator cuff strain, tendinitis and forearm muscle strain. Others are tightness and stiffness in the low back, strains in the lower and middle back, ankle sprains, and occasionally knee sprains and shin splints.

The various injuries have a variety of causes. They can be related to equipment, or court surface, or environmental conditions. Different problems will arise according to whether it is hot or cold, for instance.

Rotator cuff problems are caused by poor technique, when playing too much without sufficient flexibility and strength in the shoulder girdle area. It can also be caused by playing in windy conditions and hitting balls out of position because the ball has been carried at the last moment.

Shin splints are caused by structural problems in the foot which will give pain up the front of the legs, or by poor shoes which do not have enough shock absorption for the pounding on hard courts.

A great deal of injuries are non-preventable. Most players have to play with an injury or have some sort of problem at some time or another, but several of the niggling injuries can be prevented.

How? By playing a reasonable schedule, by not playing for too many consecutive weeks. Many players might play only two matches in a week and so can play for six weeks in a row more than likely without any problems. Others might play three or four days in a row, singles and doubles, and will probably be sore after four or five weeks. They are going to be tired – and that is when they are vulnerable.

Maintaining a good flexibility programme, making sure that you are as supple as you can be in all the different areas of the body that you use for tennis – basically, from the head to the toes – is needed.

A good stretching programme is essential and should last from 15–20 minutes before activity, and for 5–10 minutes after playing too, on a regular daily basis. Attend to problem areas more frequently with a strengthening programme, so that these areas – susceptible to strain – can be built up.

A strengthening programme is a weight-training or resistance programme. You work on your quads or your hamstrings, or whatever part is required, using machines or sand bags or an elastic tubing – whatever is available. This programme should be organized and supervised initial-

ly by somebody who knows what they are doing.

Once you have gained a significant amount of strength – enough to prevent possible injuries – you need to undertake a maintenance programme so you do not lose the gains that you have made.

A stretching programme should involve stretching all the different body parts you will be using. You can start from your head and work down to your toes, or the other way round if you prefer. Stretch all the muscle groups and also work as much as you can on the joint areas that you will be stressing.

Remember, a stretching programme should not be done from cold. You should be warm before you start so that you do not do any damage.

Stretching should always be pain free. If you are cold before you have to stretch, you should do a little skipping, jogging, or cycling on a stationary bike to raise the heart rate and body temperature. You should always go out to play or practise feeling warm. As you go out to play you should already be breaking into a sweat. There is no point to try and do that in the five minutes' knock-up before you play a match, or before you pick up a ball and start to practise.

If you have any problems, sort them out before you start playing – you could make them worse otherwise.

Tournament players who have access to someone in the field of injury prevention and care should consult them as soon as something starts to go wrong. Do not wait until it is so bad that you cannot function.

You can give yourself basic first aid for any niggle, anything that is sore, by using an ice-pack for 15–20 minutes at a time. You can use aspirin as an anti-inflammatory and for pain relief, but consult somebody if the pain does not lessen.

Ice reduces swelling, bleeding and pain and acts as a kind of anaesthetic. It is an inexpensive treatment: crush up some ice in a towel or a plastic bag, and apply with an elastic bandage or some sort of compression. (You can make ice in your freezer

211

Fig 160 A simple bandage helps to protect bruised areas.

or even use something as simple as a bag of frozen peas.)

You will often see players wearing ugly thigh bandages. They are a compression and thermal heat instrument. These bandages do not stop the problem from worsening, but they help heat up an area more quickly and keep it warm while the player is competing, whilst the compression helps to ease the soreness.

Basically, use your common sense – if you do not have to play with something that hurts, then don't. If you are going to play, then make sure you are careful in your preparation and that you stretch and warm up properly.

If you are unlucky, the basic rules of injury care and first aid are that if a new injury occurs you should use ice, elevation and compression to control the swelling and bleeding and you use rest.

If things are bad, and not getting better, go and see someone who deals in sports medicine, a doctor or physiotherapist.

29
SOME SIMPLE STRETCHING EXERCISES

The following are some simple stretching exercises which may take up a few minutes of your time, but will be of enormous benefit as they reduce tension and increase mobility. Daily stretching can keep your body from stiffening to a minimum.

Neck

Circles

Sit or stand upright with arms hanging loosely by your sides. Slowly circle your head clockwise 10 times. Repeat anticlockwise 10 times.

Forwards and Back

Postion yourself as above but drop your chin onto your chest and then lean your head back as far as possible. Do this 10 times.

Sideways

Sit upright and slowly turn your head to the right as far as possible, while keeping your head in a vertical position.

Shoulders

Arm Circles

Stand and circle both arms backwards reaching up and back as far as possible. Do 10 circles, then repeat with your arms circling forwards.

Arm behind Back

Sit or stand upright with one arm bent behind your back. Clasp your elbow (or your wrist) from behind with the opposite hand. Gently pull your elbow (or wrist) across your back and hold for 5 seconds. Repeat with the other arm.

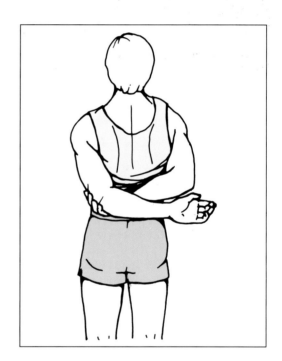

Back

Tuck

Lie on your back. Clasp your knees with both hands and pull towards your chest with a gentle rocking motion. Repeat 20 times.

Lower Back Stretch – 1

Lie on your back with knees bent and feet flat on the floor with arms out to the sides. Slowly lower both knees to the floor on the same side, then roll your knees over to touch the floor on the other side. Repeat 20 times, making sure you keep your shoulders on the floor.

Lower Back Stretch – 2

Lie on your back with one leg raised and one leg straight with arms out to your sides. Slowly lower your raised leg to the opposite hand, keeping your shoulders flat on the floor. Repeat with the other leg.

Abdominals

Lie face down on the floor. Place your palms on the floor and raise your head and arch your back. Hold the stretch for 5 seconds at first, but every few days increase the time until you can hold it for 30 seconds.

Groin

Lie flat on your back. Bend your knees and bring the heels and soles of your feet together as you pull them towards your buttocks. Let your knees fall out to the sides as widely as possible while keeping your feet in contact. Hold the stretch for 30 seconds if possible. You should eventually be able to hold the stretch for longer.

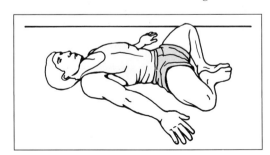

Hamstrings (Back of Leg)

Hamstring and Lower Back

Stand upright with one leg raised and resting on a chair. Keeping both legs straight and hips square, bend forward at the waist and lower your upper body onto, or towards, your raised thigh. Hold the stretch for 5–10 seconds and then come up slowly. Do this 3 times then change legs.

Quadriceps (Front of Thigh)

Flamingo Stretch

Stand upright with one hand against a wall for balance. Bend your left leg, raise your foot to your buttocks and grasp it in your left hand. Gently pull your heel towards your buttocks and hold for 5–10 seconds. Repeat with the right leg.

Note: Anyone with bad knees should take special care with this exercise.

Calf and Achilles Tendon

Push Against Wall

Stand 1–1.5m (4–5ft) from a wall. Bend one leg forward and keep the opposite leg straight. Lean against the wall while keeping your rear foot down flat and parallel to your hips. Then bend your arms, move your chest towards the wall and shift your weight forwards, so stretching the back of your lower leg. Hold the stretch for 15 seconds, then repeat with the other leg.

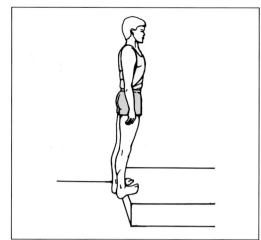

Balance on Step

Stand upright with the balls of your feet balanced on an edge or step. Slowly lower your heels toward the floor. Hold the stretch for 5–10 seconds and then relax.

Ankles

Circling

Sit or stand with one leg raised off the ground in front of you. Slowly circle your foot 20 times clockwise, then 20 times anticlockwise. Repeat with your other foot.

30
MAKING IT

What can you expect if you reach a sufficiently high standard and want to attempt a professional career? Most players step onto the professional tournament circuit at an elementary level, where the total prize money for everyone for the week is limited to $10,000. That stands in stark contrast to the top level event which may offer over $1,000,000. Life can be very tough indeed at the bottom end of the ladder and home comforts are thrown out of the window in an effort to go on the road and make it into the big time.

Jo Durie was just one of the bunch who worked hard enough to emerge from the qualifying tournaments into the world of the big money events and Grand Slam tournaments. Not only has she been ranked Number One in Britain on several occasions, but her efforts also led to her being ranked 5 in the world as she reached the semi-finals of two Grand Slam events, the French Open and the US Open. She also won a Wimbledon title – the Mixed Doubles – with Jeremy Bates and has represented Great Britain on numerous occasions at the highest level.

Here, she remembers her early days on the circuit, the hardships and struggles that any player dipping his feet in the water for the first time might expect, and the inspiration she drew both from within herself and from those around her:

After leaving school at sixteen and never having travelled abroad before, I started at the bottom of the pile of 'serious' tournaments, with the $10,000 events. I had to play qualifying and found life very difficult. We were sharing four to a room because it was cheaper. We had two single beds and two roll-away beds. The places were the cheapest we could find and we ate as cheaply as we could. We had absolutely no money at all and it was really quite tough.

It's so difficult to get any sponsorship when you are not very good. At that stage I received help from the LTA. It was usually half the air-fare and the idea was that I paid it back if I earned enough money. That was not very often to start with.

I remember it as being one long struggle, especially when you were losing week after week, as I did. When I first started having coaching from Alan I went to America for seven weeks and did not win a match.

That was in the days of the Avon Futures tour. They were like qualifying tournaments for the main tour, because if you reached the semi-finals, you were promoted to the main tour for two weeks and then it was up to you to prove yourself at the higher level.

So, I started off in the Futures, which was the highest level before the main tour, and then the next week I was in qualifying for the Futures and spent two weeks there losing in the first round. Then I had to go down to another level to pre-qualifying (where anyone could turn up and have a go) and I did not win a match. After just three weeks there I wanted to come home, but I stuck it out with everybody else.

What kept me going was my belief that I could be better than everybody else, and I could not really understand why I was not beating them at the time. It was puzzling me more than anything else. I knew I wasn't practising very well (which is a huge factor in improving anyone's tennis!) and that if I did start practising better and got fitter, then I would definitely win more. I knew I had the talent in there and could hit the ball hard.

I was so puzzled about it all that I stayed. That and the fact that it would have cost too much money to go back home! I had my flight booked on a cheap ticket and to change it would have meant buying a completely new one. There was no way I could afford it. I was trapped really, and had to keep going.

So things were tough, but the good thing was that we all helped each other. We were all lumped into the same position and everybody knew how tough it was. Everyone was a bit homesick. There was a whole crowd of us and we used to play games like Scrabble and Monopoly before and after our matches and go out for a drink if we could. We travelled everywhere together, so there were a lot of people you could become friendly with. I don't think that happens on the main tour, especially nowadays with tennis becoming big business and with most players having friends or coaches travelling with them.

After the abortive first attempt I went back to the same Avon tour a year later. I started off in the Futures and in the first weeks I reached the semi-finals, which meant I qualified for the main tournament the following week. I always remember that it was in Kansas City and on the way there the airline lost my suitcase. I had to play Betty Stove in the first round and I had no clothes at all, but she kindly lent me some of her own.

On the plus side I remember there was someone at the airport to meet me, I was in a nice hotel with a cut rate that wasn't expensive and I only had to share with one other girl. We had lunch given to us, meal tickets and I remember that I had a voucher to get a free pair of boots from a local shop. We were also taken on a sight-seeing trip and it was cars here and cars there. It was a different world and I was a bit over-whelmed to start with. We had ball boys and linesmen everywhere and quite a decent crowd watching and I thought: 'This is the life.' It makes you think that all the hard times of trying to get around without much money were worthwhile after all.

I felt pleased that I'd actually made it. It was like a carrot dangling, saying: 'Look, this is what you get if you not only play well, but practise and train.'

But it didn't last long, because I lost in the first round there in Kansas and also the next week. So, I had to go back down to the Futures, in Boise, Idaho and start all over again.

The funny thing was that I came back down to the qualifying and some of the players there were a little resentful of me. That surprised me, because I thought they'd say it was great getting up there. However, that just gave me more incentive to go for the main tour, and the week after I qualified again and found myself in Los Angeles. I stayed at an unbelievable place, right on the ocean, and it really gave me the incentive to stay up there.

When you reach the top level and you think the struggle is over, there's a different kind of pressure. You realize that suddenly you are on your own. Up to now, you have probably been thinking it doesn't matter and you win some and you lose some. Now, everyone is looking at you to win and that is very different because when you come off court it's not a case of, 'Oh, bad luck. She played well.' It's, 'How could you lose to her? Is there something wrong with you?' Suddenly the questions are very different to what you've experienced before. The same things even happen with your friends. Suddenly they think you are a great tennis player, when really you have just scrambled your way into the main tour and you're hanging on to try and stay there.

You put pressure on yourself to keep performing at your best, which is silly because usually you can only perform at your average. Your best only comes along once in a while. I expected to be playing well every week, but I found out it's impossible to achieve your best every match. What you really need in tennis is a very good basic average. That has to get you through a lot of matches and I think you come to realize that after a while . . .

The Avon Futures tour does not exist as

such now. There is no automatic 'promotion' if you do well. But there are stepping stones from the $10,000 tournaments and you earn you entry into the bigger events by virtue of your computer ranking.

It is a slow and often frustrating process, but everyone – as Jo points out – is in the same position. The path to those 'unbelievable places on the ocean' lies in hard work and dedication. Everyone is after the same thing and it is up to you to prove you are the best.

I have done my bit. Hopefully within the pages of this book I have given you a cross-section of ideas with which to go out, experiment with and have fun.

Remember, be aware at all times that tennis is a fun game and that even in the heat of battle you can get pleasure from competing.

If you can develop a feeling of enjoyment, I am sure you will feel much more comfortable and will be rewarded with a better performance.

Bear in mind that tennis is not a static game – it is a very mobile, agile sport. When practising, remember that good footwork and good anticipation will lend themselves to producing a better technique.

You so often hear – not just in tennis, but in all walks of life – people saying, 'If only I had worked a little bit harder, if only I had listened better, if only I had practised harder.' Don't let that be part of your vocabulary. Go out and find time to practise, diligently and seriously, and you will reap the rewards by developing and improving your game.

APPENDIX I

Short Tennis

Short Tennis was first introduced in Sweden, and since 1980 it has found a place in thousands of schools and clubs throughout the UK. There are even Short Tennis tournaments organized on a county level.

The idea of the game is to introduce the skills, atmosphere and competition of tennis, especially to those too young to be able to wield a full-size racquet and without the power to hit a conventional ball. Short Tennis can be played by anyone from five years of age and it can be played indoors or outdoors.

Part of the Lawn Tennis Association (LTA)'s development programme, Short Tennis encourages children at a young age to develop an interest in tennis without being overwhelmed by the complexities of the 'real' game. It is, if you like, a stepping stone to the real thing and it helps young players to acquire technique naturally and without stress.

They can learn all the normal skills, such as hand–eye co-ordination, the backhand and forehand, the serve, the volley and the smash and the technique for racquet and ball skills is exactly the same as for normal tennis.

Short Tennis is played with a light plastic racquet and a soft, spongy ball. Heavier balls are then available for the more advanced player. The court is the same size as that used for badminton, which is 13.4× 6.1m (44×20ft). The net should be 80cm (2ft 7in) high.

Method

An ideal way to start teaching the sport is to ask the player to bounce the ball up and down on the ground. From there, ask him to turn the racquet between each bounce. Then introduce movement as well as ball control. Set up a cone and ask the pupil to run to it while bouncing the ball off the racquet into the air and then off the floor on the return trip. If several players are available, split them into teams to enhance the fun of competition.

The next stage is learning to rally. Ask pupils to hit the ball against a wall, up to ten times to begin with, then introduce some movement, once again by standing across the net with the pupils lined up along the other side. Let them volley the ball back to you then run around behind you and so back into the line for the next turn.

Encourage pupil involvement by asking them to take turns hand-feeding the ball over the net. Then, get them to actually rally. They are replaced when either a target is reached (say, 10 strokes) or the ball is missed.

The serve comes next, beginning under-arm and then progressing to over-arm, tossing the ball up and throwing – directing – the racquet at the ball. Nothing fancy, just hitting the ball over the net.

Volleying can be taught by asking one pupil to throw the ball over the net while another 'punches' it back – with the racquet of course! Then, move on to rallying.

Matches can now be played, on a first-to-11 basis, with a two-point margin needed to win. The rules are the same as for the normal game. The ball can be served over- or under-arm and the service is alternated between the players every two points. The change of ends comes after every eight points. The rules for doubles are the same.

The equipment for Short Tennis is available from dealers throughout the country (*see* Appendix II, Useful Addresses).

APPENDIX II

Useful Addresses

UK

The Lawn Tennis Association
The Queen's Club
West Kensington
London WA14 9EG
Tel: 071 385 2366
Fax: 071 381 5965

The Professional Tennis Coaches Association
21, Glencairn Court
Lansdown Road
Cheltenham
Gloucestershire GL50 2NB
Tel: 0242 524 701

The International Tennis Federation
Palliser Road
Baron's Court
London W14 9EN
Tel: 071 381 8060
Fax: 071 381 3989

For details of your nearest stockist of Short Tennis equipment, call (0924) 828 222. A video and teachers' guide to Short Tennis are both available from The Lawn Tennis Association.

Australia

Tennis Australia
Private Bag 6060
Richmond South 3121
Victoria
Tel: 613 655 1277
Fax: 613 650 2743

Canada

Tennis Canada
3111 Steeles Avenue West
Downsview
Ontario M3J 3H2
Tel: 416 665 9777
Fax: 416 665 9017

France

Fédération Française de Tennis
Stade Roland Garros
2, Avenue Gordon Bennett
75016 Paris
Tel: 331 4743 4800

Germany

Deutscher Tennis Bund
Hallerstrasse 89
2000 Hamburg 13
Tel: 4940 41178-Z

Italy

Federazione Italiana Tennis
Viale Tiziano 70
00196 Rome
Tel: 396 396 0092/39 66 743

Spain

Rea Federacion Espanola de Tennis
Avenida Diagonal 618-3D
08201 Barcelona
Tel: 343 200 5355/201 0844

USA

United States Tennis Association Inc.
12th Floor
1212 Avenue of the Americas
New York NY 10036
Tel: 212 302 3322
Fax: 212 764 1838

Addresses and phone numbers of countries not covered in this list can be found by phoning or writing to the International Tennis Federation (*see* UK addresses).

GLOSSARY

Australian formation A tactical ploy used in doubles by the server and his partner (*see* page 196).

Backscratch Position achieved by the raquet during the service action prior to the delivery of the raquet to the ball. The raquet will be positioned as if you were scratching your back with the raquet.

Ball sense The ability to understand the movement of the ball, which enables you to get in position to execute a shot.

Baseliner A tennis player that will be rallying from behind the baseline.

Block shot A stroke where there is almost no motion used with the raquet.

Conversion zone An imaginary area within approximately 60–90cm (2–3ft) of either side of the service line.

Delicate shots These are shots that require a very sensitive touch and caressing of the ball, such as drop shots, drop volleys and the volley lob.

Dink A shot where you absorb almost all the pace of the ball coming towards you – it is a volley technique adapted to groundstroke play.

Drills Exercises that are devised to perfect technique, stamina, consistency, control and tactics.

Early ball The striking of the ball at the top of the bounce or even on the way up from the ground.

Elevation Achieved by naturally allowing weight transference to lift you off the ground whilst playing a shot.

Feel shot *See* delicate shots.

Floating return A shot which will travel slowly through the air with a higher than normal net clearance.

Grand Slam The four major championships of the world. The Australian Open, French Open, US Open and Wimbledon.

Groundstroker A tennis player who will be striking the ball after it has contacted the playing surface, i.e., after the ball has bounced.

Hand skills The ability within the execution of the stroke to add subtle changes to the intended direction of the ball by closing or opening and thus offering the angle of the raquet face with last-moment hand adjustments.

Hip pivot The hip pivot is a position achieved when preparing to play a stroke. On completing the backswing to your stroke, your feet should be square to the net. However, your hips should have moved approx 45° back with the playing arm, creating the hip pivot. This is a powerful position to be in, ready to transfer your weight into the shot.

Liquid rhythm You have to be 'slinky'; your body has to be very supple to get a feel of spreading *in* the movement.

Moonball A tactic used when two players are playing from the baseline and one uses the lob as a rallying groundstroke.

Moving around the ball This is the ability to move with small steps to create the required space for the correct position to strike the ball.

Non-playing arm The arm that has no role in striking the ball. (Naturally, this does not apply to double-handers.)

Off-shot This is a shot where there is sufficient time to play a forehand when the ball is travelling to your backhand wing, or vice versa. You will be striking the ball early and aggressively in a direction *opposite to the cross-court shot*.

Playing to length A tactical ploy when you endeavour to keep the shots you are playing as deep as possible into your opponent's court.

Raquet control The ability to consistently apply the raquet face to the ball without loss of control.

Ready position The balanced position achieved between each shot prior to the particular shot you are about to execute.

Shape of strokes An individual's interpretation of preparing, striking and following through whilst playing his strokes.

Short Tennis A modified game of tennis devised for juniors which will introduce youngsters to the game. Short Tennis uses a sponge ball, a small court and small raquets.

Soft touch *See* delicate shots.

Strike zone or impact zone The space which a player creates, when preparing to play his shots by moving his feet accordingly to strike the ball.

Threes A specialized training routine generally dynamic, naturally involving three players.

Throwing action During the service action when the raquet is projected at the ball from the backscratch position. This is called throwing the raquet head at the ball.

Tie-break When a set is drawn at six games all, the tie-break is introduced to settle the set. The winner of the tie-break wins the set 7 games to 6.

Weight of shot This is a term which describes the pace of the ball from the raquet.

Wrist snap Occurs during the service action just prior to the raquet head striking the ball. The server is seeking extra speed or spin by snapping the wrist aggressively just before impact.